THE APOCRYPHAL GOSPEL
OF ST PETER

ΚΑΙΕ̣ΑΝ...ΤΗ...ΕΚΕΙΒΕ...Ο...ΡΑΟϹΕ...
ΚΑΙΕΠΙϹΑ...ΠΑϹ...ΠΕΦΩ ΟΔΕΚΑΘΩ ϹΕΚΕΑ
ΕΙΕ̣Ε̣Η...ΜΕΝΟϹΕΠΠΙϹΘΡΑΦΕΩ ΤΑΡΚΝ...
ΕΤΕΛΩΠ...ΕΤΕΡ...Π...ΡΟϹΚΥΟΤΕ...Ο ϹΕΤΕΡ...
ΚΑΙΑΜΦΟΤΕΡΟΙΟΙΝ...ΕΚΕΙϹΟΤΙΚ...Ν...
ΟΙΝΟΙϹΤΡΑΛΙΤΗ ΕΚΓΝΟΙ ΕϹΤΟΝΚΩΝΤΟ...
ΡΙΩΝΑΚΑΠΟΥϹΤΡΕϹΚΗ ΠΡΟΥϹΤΕΡΗ ϹΩΝ...
ΦΙΛΑϹϹΟΝΤΕϹΚΑΙΕΖΗΤΟ ΠΑΥΤ...Ν ΑΥΤΩΝ...
ΤΟ ΤΗΝΟΡΑϹΙΝΕΩϹ...ΒΟΝΤ ϹΑΠΟΤΟΥΤΕΦΟΥ ΤΡΕΙϹ
ΟΝΔΡΕϹΚΑΤΟΥϹ ΑΠΟΤΟΝ ΕΝΑΠ...ΒΟΙ...
ϹΤΑΥΡΟΝ ΑΚΟΛΟΘΟΥΝ...ΑΥΤΟΙϹΚΑΙΤΗΠΡ...Ν ΤΟ
ΤΗΝΚΕΦΑΛΗΝ ΧΩ... ...ΜΕΧΡΙΤΟ ΤΟΥΡΑΝΟΥ
ΤΟΥΔΕΧΕΙ ΡΑΓΩΤΟΥ...ΟΥΠΤΑΝΤΩΝ ΤΗΝ ΚΥΡΙΟΝ
ϹΑΠΤΟΥ ΟΥΡΑΝΟΥϹΚΑΙΦΩΝΗΚΟΤΕΝΕΙϹΤΩ...
ΟΤΙΡΩΜΗΧΕΤΙϹ...ϹΕΚΗΡΥΖΕϹΤΟΙΚϹΙΝ...ΚΑΙ...
ΥΠΗΚΟΥϹΗΚΟΝΕΤΟΑΠΟΤΟΥϹΤΑΥΡΟΝΤΗΝΑΙΪϹΟΡΕ
ΕΚΑΠΤΤΟΝΤΟΟΥΝ...Η...ΟΙϹΕΝ...ΟΙ...ΤΟ...

ΚΑΙ ΕΝΕΓΚΩΝ ... ΤΩΝ ΣΤΡΑΤΙΩΤΩΝ ... ΤΟΝ ΛΑΟΝ ... ΟΥΚ ... ΕΠΕΙΔΗ ΠΟΟΥΝΕ
... ΟΝΤΑΙ ... ΝΟΙ ΑΛΛΑ ΕΝΤΕΣΣΟΙ ΟΥΡΑΝΩΙ
... ΟΣ ΚΑΙ ΕΛΘΟΝ ΚΑΙ ΕΙΣ ΕΛΘΩΝ ΕΙΣ ΤΟ ΜΝΗΜΑ
... ΔΟΝΤΕΣ ΟΠΕΡ ΤΟΝ ΚΕΝΤΥΡΙΩΝ ΝΥΚΤΟΣ ΕΠΕΛΕΝ
... ΕΙ ΤΟΝ ... ΕΝ ΤΕ ΤΟΝ ΤΑΦΟΝ ΟΝ ΕΦΥΛΑΣΣΟΝ ΚΑΙ
... ΑΥΤΟ ... ΕΙΔΟΝ ΑΝΟΙ ... ΕΣ ΜΕΓΑ
... ΓΟΝΤΕΣ ... ΥΙΟΣ ΗΝ ΘΥ ΑΠΟΚΡΙΘΕΙΣ Ο ΠΕΙΛΑΤΟΣ
ΕΦΗ ΕΓΩ ΚΑΘΑΡΕΥΩ ΤΟΥ ΑΙΜΑΤΟΣ ΤΟΥ ΥΙΟΥ ΤΟΥ ΘΕΟΥ ΥΜΙΝ ΔΕ
ΤΟΥΤΟ ΕΔΟΞΕΝ ΕΙΤΑ ΠΡΟΣΕΛΘΟΝΤΕΣ ΠΑΝΤΕΣ ΕΔΕΟΝΤΟ ΑΥΤΟΥ
ΚΑΙ ΠΑΡΕΚΑΛΟΥΝ ΚΑΙ ΕΝ ΤΩ ΚΕΝΤΥΡΙΩΝΙ ΚΑΙ ΤΟΙΣ ΣΤΡΑΤΙΩ
ΤΑΙΣ ... ΕΙ ΕΙΝΑΙ ΕΔΟΝ ... ΕΙ ΜΗ ΣΥΜΦΕΡΕΙ ΓΑΡ ΦΗΣΙΝ ΗΜΙΝ
ΟΦΛΗΣΑΙ ΜΕΓΙΣΤΗΝ ΑΜΑΡΤΙΑΝ ΕΜΠΡΟΣΘΕΝ ΤΟΥ ΘΕΟΥ
ΚΑΙ ΜΗ ... ΣΕΙΝ ... ΠΑΡΑ ΤΟΥ ΛΑΟΥ ΤΩΝ ΙΟΥΔΑΙΩΝ
ΚΑΙ ΛΙΘΑΣΘΗΝΑΙ ΕΚΕΛΕΥΣΕΝ ΟΥΝ Ο ΠΕΙΛΑΤΟΣ ΤΩΝ ΚΕΝ
ΤΥΡΙΩΝ ΚΑΙ ΤΟΙΣ ΣΤΡΑΤΙΩΤΑΙΣ ΜΗΔΕΝ ΕΙΠΕΙΝ ΟΙ ΘΥ ... ΔΕ
... ΚΑΙ Η ΜΑΡΙΑ Η ΜΑΓΔΑΛΗΝΗ ΜΑΘΗΤΡΙΑ ΤΟΥ ΚΥ
ΦΟΒΟΥΜΕΝΗ ΔΙΑ ΤΟΥΣ ΙΟΥΔΑΙΟΥΣ ΕΠΕΙΔΗ ΕΦΛΕΓΟΝΤΟ

ΕΥΑΓΓΕΛΙΟΝ ΚΑΤΑ ΠΕΤΡΟΝ

THE AKHMÎM FRAGMENT

OF THE

APOCRYPHAL GOSPEL OF ST PETER

EDITED

WITH AN INTRODUCTION NOTES AND INDICES

BY

H. B. SWETE, D.D

HON LITT D DUBLIN

FELLOW OF GONVILLE AND CAIUS COLLEGE

REGIUS PROFESSOR OF DIVINITY, CAMBRIDGE

WIPF & STOCK · Eugene, Oregon

Wipf and Stock Publishers
199 W 8th Ave, Suite 3
Eugene, OR 97401

The Akhmîm Fragment of the Apocryphal Gospel of St. Peter
Edited with Introduction Notes and Indices
By Swete, Henry Barclay
Softcover ISBN-13: 978-1-6667-0427-3
Hardcover ISBN-13: 978-1-6667-0428-0
eBook ISBN-13: 978-1-6667-0429-7
Publication date 3/3/2021
Previously published by Macmillan and Co., 1893

AT the end of November, 1892, shortly after the appearance of M. Bouriant's *editio princeps*, I published for the use of students a tentatively corrected text of the newly discovered fragment of the Petrine Gospel This reprint was issued again in February, 1893, with some corrections obtained from the MS. through the kindness of the late Professor Bensly, whose recent death has brought upon all studies of this kind a loss which it is impossible to estimate The text which I now offer to the public has been revised throughout by the aid of the heliographic reproduction of the MS just published by M. Ernest Leroux of Paris. Through the courtesy of M. Leroux I am able to enrich my book with a specimen of this facsimile

The Introduction and the notes which have been added to the text are based on lectures delivered in the Divinity School at Cambridge during the Lent Term of the present year. The results at which I have ventured to arrive were reached independently, but in preparing my materials for the press I have freely availed myself of all the literature upon the subject which has fallen into my hands It is difficult to discriminate in all cases between details which have suggested themselves directly and those which have been gathered from other sources; but I have endeavoured to acknowledge, in passing, the most important of the debts of which I am conscious

The suggestive lecture of Professor J. Armitage Robinson, which appeared almost immediately after my reprint of M. Bouriant's text, and Professor A. Harnack's edition of the Petrine fragments, assisted me in the earlier part of my investigation, if I am less indebted to Professor Th. Zahn's *Evangelium des Petrus*, it is because nearly the whole of the following pages was in type before the publication of Dr Zahn's work To Mr J Rendel Harris, Reader in Palaeography at Cambridge, I owe not only many valuable suggestions during the progress of my book, but much kind assistance in the final correction of the proofs.

CAMBRIDGF,

May, 1893

CONTENTS

ὁ τῶν ἀπάντων τεχνίτης λόγος ὁ καθήμενος ἐπὶ τῶν χερουβὶμ καὶ συνέχων τὰ πάντα, φανερωθεὶς τοῖς ἀνθρώποις, ἔδωκεν ἡμῖν τετράμορφον τὸ εὐαγγέλιον, ἑνὶ δὲ πνεύματι συνεχόμενον

INTRODUCTION.

I.

Eusebius[1] enumerates six works attributed to St Peter—two Epistles, a Gospel, an Apocalypse, a book of Acts, and a Preaching He regards the first Epistle as undoubtedly genuine, the second as not definitely canonical, the rest of the Petrine writings are distinctly outside the Canon, and the Gospel is of heretical origin.

His judgement is based on the general opinion of the Church While the first Epistle was acknowledged on all hands and the second was widely used, no Church writer had appealed to the Petrine Gospel, Acts, Preaching, or Apocalypse.

[1] *H E* iii 3 Πέτρου μὲν οὖν ἐπιστολὴ μία ἡ λεγομένη αὐτοῦ προτέρα ἀνωμολόγηται τὴν δὲ φερομένην αὐτοῦ δευτέραν οὐκ ἐνδιάθηκον μὲν εἶναι παρειλήφαμεν, ὅμως δὲ πολλοῖς χρήσιμος φανεῖσα μετὰ τῶν ἄλλων ἐσπουδάσθη γραφῶν τό γε μὴν τῶν ἐπικεκλημένων αὐτοῦ Πράξεων καὶ τὸ κατ' αὐτὸν ὠνομασμένον Εὐαγγέλιον, τό τε λεγόμενον αὐτοῦ Κήρυγμα καὶ τὴν καλουμένην Ἀποκάλυψιν, οὐδ' ὅλως ἐν καθολικοῖς ἴσμεν παραδεδομένα ὅτι μήτε ἀρχαίων μήτε τῶν καθ' ἡμᾶς τις ἐκκλησιαστικὸς συγγραφεὺς ταῖς ἐξ αὐτῶν συνεχρήσατο μαρτυρίαις Comp iii 25 τῶν δὲ ἀντιλεγομένων γνωρίμων δ' οὖν ὅμως τοῖς πολλοῖς. ἡ Πέτρου δευτέρα ἐπιστολή ἐν τοῖς νόθοις κατατετάχθω ἡ ἀποκάλυψις Πέτρου τὸν κατάλογον πεποιήμεθα . . ἵν' εἰδέναι ἔχοιμεν αὐτάς τε ταύτας [the canonical writings, and the *antilegomena*], καὶ τὰς ὀνόματι τῶν ἀποστόλων πρὸς τῶν αἱρετικῶν

προφερομένας, ἤτοι ὡς Πέτρου καὶ Θωμᾶ καὶ Ματθία, ἢ καί τινων παρὰ τούτους ἄλλων εὐαγγέλια περιεχούσας . . ὧν οὐδὲν οὐδαμῶς ἐν συγγράμματι τῶν κατὰ τὰς διαδοχὰς ἐκκλησιαστικῶν τις ἀνὴρ εἰς μνήμην ἀγαγεῖν ἠξίωσεν Jerome adds a seventh book, the ' Judgement '; in his estimate of the Petrine literature he follows Eusebius but treads with a firmer step *de uirr. illustr.* 1 Simon Petrus . scripsit duas epistolas quae catholicae nominantur, quarum secunda a plerisque eius negatur propter stili cum priore dissonantiam. sed et Euangelium iuxta Marcum, qui auditor eius et interpres fuit, huius dicitur libri autem e quibus unus Actorum eius inscribitur, alius Euangelii, tertius Praedicationis, quartus Ἀποκαλύψεως, quintus Iudicii, inter apocryphas scripturas repudiantur.

S P.

b

Of the Gospel, before the recovery of the Akhmîm fragment, not a single sentence was known to have survived. Origen indeed asserts that those who held the Brethren of the Lord to have been sons of Joseph by a first wife, based their theory upon either the Gospel of Peter or the "Book of James[1]." Beyond this precarious testimony the only reference to the Petrine Gospel by writers earlier than Eusebius is to be found in a fragment of Serapion preserved in another part of the *Ecclesiastical History*[2]. Serapion was eighth Bishop of Antioch, succeeding Maximinus and himself succeeded by Asclepiades[3]. It has been shewn by Bishop Lightfoot that Serapion's episcopate began between A D. 189 and 192 : the year of his death is less certain, but he seems to have been still living during the persecution of the Church by Septimius Severus (A D. 202—3)[4] On the whole his period of episcopal activity may safely be placed in the last decade of the second century. This Serapion had left a treatise relating to the Gospel of Peter from which Eusebius quotes a few sentences. It appears to have been a pastoral letter addressed to the clergy or people of Rhosus, consisting of a general criticism of the Gospel followed by extracts from it. The passage preserved by Eusebius explains the circumstances under which the letter was written In the course of a visit to Rhosus the Bishop of Antioch learnt that some bitterness had arisen between members of the Church upon the question of the public use of the Gospel of Peter He glanced over its pages, and not suspecting the existence of any heretical tendency at Rhosus, authorised the reading of the book. After his departure information reached him

---

[1] *Comm in Matt* t. x. 17. τοὺς δὲ ἀδελφοὺς Ἰησοῦ φασι τινες εἶναι, ἐκ παραδόσεως ὁρμώμενοι τοῦ ἐπιγεγραμμένου Κατὰ Πέτρον εὐαγγελίου, ἢ τῆς βίβλου Ἰακώβου, υιοὺς Ἰωσὴφ ἐκ προτέρας γυναικὸς συνῳκηκυίας αὐτῷ πρὸ τῆς Μαρίας.

[2] *H E.* vi. 12 ἡμεῖς γάρ, ἀδελφοί, καὶ Πέτρον καὶ τοὺς ἄλλους ἀποστόλους ἀποδεχόμεθα ὡς Χριστόν τὰ δὲ ὀνόματι αὐτῶν ψευδεπίγραφα ὡς ἔμπειροι παραιτούμεθα, γινώσκοντες ὅτι τὰ τοιαῦτα οὐ παρελάβομεν. ἐγὼ γὰρ γενόμενος παρ' ὑμῖν ὑπενόουν τοὺς πάντας ὀρθῇ πίστει προσφέρεσθαι καὶ μὴ διελθὼν τὸ ὑπ' αὐτῶν προφερόμενον ὀνόματι Πέτρου εὐαγγέλιον, εἶπον ὅτι Εἰ τοῦτό ἐστι μόνον τὸ δοκοῦν ὑμῖν παρέχειν μικροψυχίαν, ἀναγινωσκέσθω   νῦν δὲ μαθὼν ὅτι αἱρέσει τινὶ ὁ νοῦς αὐτῶν ἐνεφώλευεν ἐκ τῶν

λεχθέντων μοι, σπουδάσω πάλιν γενέσθαι πρὸς ὑμᾶς· ὥστε, ἀδελφοί, προσδοκᾶτέ με ἐν τάχει ἡμεῖς (fort. leg. ὑμεῖς) δέ, ἀδελφοί, καταλαβόμενοι ὁποίας ἦν αἱρέσεως ὁ Μαρκιανός, καὶ ἑαυτῷ ἠναντιοῦτο μὴ νοῶν ἃ ἐλάλει, ἃ μαθήσεσθε (fort leg ὡς καὶ ἑαυτῷ ἠναντ μὴ ν. ἃ ἐλάλει, μαθήσεσθε) ἐξ ὧν ὑμῖν ἐγράφη ἐδυνήθημεν γὰρ παρ' ἄλλων τῶν ἀσκησάντων αὐτὸ τοῦτο εὐαγγέλιον, τουτέστι παρὰ τῶν διαδόχων τῶν καταρξαμένων αὐτοῦ, οὓς Δοκητὰς καλοῦμεν—τὰ γὰρ πλείονα φρονήματα ἐκείνων ἐστὶ τῆς διδασκαλίας—χρησάμενοι παρ' αὐτῶν διελθεῖν, καὶ εὑρεῖν τὰ μὲν πλείονα τοῦ ὀρθοῦ λόγου τοῦ Σωτῆρος, τινὰ δὲ προσδιεσταλμένα, ἃ καὶ ὑπετάξαμεν ὑμῖν

[3] *H E.* v 19, 22, vi 18.

[4] *Ignatius*, ii p. 459 ff.

which threw a new light upon the matter and determined him to visit Rhosus again without delay. He had learnt that the Gospel had originated among a party known to Catholic Christians as the *Docetae*, and was still in use among that party, who appear to have been led at Rhosus by one Marcianus[1], and on procuring a copy of the Gospel from other members of the party and examining it in detail, he had found that the book, although generally sound, contained certain accretions of another character, specimens of which he proceeded to give.

Rhosus was at a later date one of the sees of Cilicia Secunda[2], a Bishop of Rhosus signed the synodical letter of the Council of Antioch in A.D. 363[3]. At the end of the second century the town probably had no Bishop of its own, in any case it was under the authority of the great neighbouring see of Antioch, whose later patriarchal jurisdiction included both Cilicias[4] Rhosus stood just inside the bay of Issus (the modern Gulf of Iskenderun), to the south-west, fifty miles off, lay the extremity of the long arm of Cyprus, Antioch was not above thirty miles to the south east, but lofty hills, a continuation of the range of Amanus, prevented direct communication with the capital. It was in this obscure dependency of the great Syrian see that the Petrine Gospel first attracted notice. To Serapion it was clearly unknown till he saw it at Rhosus. Yet Serapion was not only Bishop of the most important see in the East, but a man of considerable activity in letters, and a controversialist[5]. It is natural to infer that the circulation of the Gospel before A D 190 was very limited, and probably confined to the party from which it emanated Even at Rhosus an attempt to use it as a Church book had provoked opposition. When Serapion wished to procure a copy, he succeeded in doing so only through the favour or indiscretion of some who belonged to the party. All this points to a narrow sphere of influence, and Serapion's censure would assuredly have checked the use of the book in the diocese of Antioch This inference is confirmed by the extreme scantiness of subsequent references to the Petrine Gospel It is mentioned by only four writers in the next three centuries, and no personal knowledge of the book is implied in their notices. The testimony of Origen, Eusebius, and Jerome has been quoted already Theodoret must be added to them, but his statement that the Gospel according to Peter was used by the Nazarenes is hard to reconcile with Serapion's first-hand account of its tendencies[6] There

[1] The Armenian version gives *Marcion* (Robinson, p. 14), but the change has little inherent probability

[2] Ramsay, *Asia Minor*, p. 386

[3] Socr iii 25 Mansi, iii. 372.

[4] Neale, *Holy Eastern Church*, i 1. 6.

[5] *H. E* v 19, vi 12.

[6] Theodoret *haer fabb.* ii 2 οἱ δὲ Να-

is a yet greater dearth of evidence in the ancient catalogues of Biblical writings.   Even those among them which include certain apocryphal books are with one exception silent as to the Petrine Gospel   The Petrine Apocalypse finds honourable mention in the Muratorian fragment and in three other lists, the Gospel is mentioned only in the *notitia librorum apocryphorum* attached to the Gelasian *Decretum de libris recipiendis et non recipiendis*[1]   This document was first attributed to Gelasius by Hincmar of Rheims, and though it probably contains older elements, in its present form it cannot be placed earlier than the eighth or ninth century; whether its reference to the Gospel of Peter is to be traced to the words of Jerome, or points to the circulation of a Latin version in Western Europe at the beginning of the middle ages, must for the present remain uncertain.   The latter alternative is not impossible.   The Manicheans of Africa and the West prided themselves on the possession of numerous *apocrypha*, some of which appear to have belonged to the Petrine group[2].

There is no reason to doubt that the Akhmîm fragment was rightly assigned by M. Bouriant to the lost Gospel of Peter   It claims to belong to a personal narrative by that Apostle, and it formed, so far as we can judge, a part of a complete Gospel and not merely of a history of the Passion, for it assumes an acquaintance on the part of its readers with such circumstances as the choice of the Twelve, the names and occupation of two of them, and their connexion with Galilee   Its tendency is, moreover, in harmony with Serapion's account of the Petrine Gospel   Our Lord is invariably called ὁ κύριος or ὁ υἱὸς τοῦ θεοῦ.   He undergoes Crucifixion without suffering pain, His risen Body assumes supernatural proportions.   These and other particulars are at least consistent with a Docetic origin, yet our fragment is orthodox in its general tone, as Serapion admits the Docetic Gospel

---

ζωραῖοι ᾿Ιουδαῖοί εἰσι τὸν Χριστὸν τιμῶντες ὡς ἄνθρωπον δίκαιον καὶ τῷ καλουμένῳ Κατὰ Πέτρον εὐαγγελίῳ κεχρημένοι   According to Epiphanius (xxix 9) the Nazarenes used the Hebrew ' Matthew' (ἔχουσι δὲ τὸ κατὰ Ματθαῖον εὐαγγέλιον πληρέστατον ᾿Εβραιστί)   Eusebius says of the Ebionites (*H E* iii 27) εὐαγγελίῳ δὲ μόνῳ τῷ καθ᾿ ῾Εβραίους λεγομένῳ χρώμενοι τῶν λοιπῶν σμικρὸν ἐποιοῦντο λόγον.   If the Nazarenes really circulated the Petrine Gospel, the fact was possibly due to its anti-Judaic tone ; cf Epiph. 1 c πάνυ

δὲ οὗτοι ἐχθροὶ τοῖς ᾿Ιουδαίοις ὑπάρχουσιν.

[1] Migne, *P. L* lix
[2] Comp Philastr. *haer* 88 habent Manichaei apocrypha beati Andreae apostoli   et alii tales Andreae beati et Ioannis Actus euangelistae, beati et Petri similiter apostoli Aug *c. Faust.* xxx. 4, where Faustus says, Mitto enim ceteros eiusdem domini nostri apostolos Petrum et Andream, Thomam et . Ioannem sed hos quidem ut dixi praetereo quia eos uos exclusistis ex canone.

to have been. Lastly, it bears internal evidence of belonging to a work of the second century Its style and character resemble those of other second century *apocrypha*, and it has a note of comparative simplicity and sobriety which is wanting in apocryphal writings of a later date

II

We may now proceed to examine the contents of the fragment. It covers a portion of the Gospel history roughly corresponding to Matt XXVII 24—XXVIII 15 = Mark XV 15—XVI 8 = Luke XXIII. 24—XXIV. 10 = John XIX 13— XX 12 A superficial comparison shews that the Petrine account is considerably the longest of the five, and exceeds by about one fourth the average length of the four canonical narratives

In what relation does this new and longest history of the Passion stand to the Four Gospels? For minute details the reader is referred to the notes attached to the text, for the present it will be necessary only to point out the general results

1. The Petrine Passion-history relates a large number of circumstances which are not to be found in any canonical Gospel The following are the most important of the new incidents

(*a*) Herod and the Jewish judges of the Lord abstain from washing their hands after Pilate's example

(*b*) The order for the Crucifixion is given by Herod.

(*c*) At this juncture Joseph, who is a friend of Pilate, seeks permission to bury the Body and is referred by Pilate to Herod. Herod replies that the Body would in any case be buried before sunset, in accordance with the Jewish law

(*d*) Herod then delivers the Lord to the people, who push Him before them exclaiming, *Let us hale the Son of God.* They set Him on a seat of Judgement saying, *Judge righteously, thou King of Israel.* Some prick Him with a reed, others scourge Him saying, *Thus let us honour the Son of God.*

(*e*) At the moment of crucifixion He is silent, as free from pain.

(*f*) The Cross is erected, the garments are spread on the ground beneath it.

(*g*) The censure of the penitent malefactor is turned upon the crucifiers, who revenge themselves by directing that his legs shall not be broken, with the view of prolonging his sufferings.

(*h*) The Jews regard the darkness which envelopes Judaea at noonday as indicating that the sun has already set, and carry lamps as in the night; some of them fall.

(*i*) At this point they offer the Lord gall mingled with vinegar, apparently for the purpose of hastening His Death

(*j*) The Lord is taken up after uttering the loud cry *My Power, My Power, thou hast forsaken Me*

(*k*) The nails are drawn forth from the Hands, and the Body is laid on the earth. The earthquake ensues ; the sun then shines out again, and it is found to be the ninth hour.

(*l*) The Jews in their joy give the Body to Joseph, who washes it The tomb in which it is laid is known as 'Joseph's Garden.'

(*m*) Presently the joy is turned into general mourning The people beat their breasts exclaiming *He was righteous ,* their leaders cry *Woe to our sins !* the disciples, suspected of designs upon the Temple, seek a place of concealment. Meanwhile they keep up their fast until the Sabbath

(*n*) With the assistance of a military guard under the command of the centurion Petronius, the Jewish leaders roll a stone to the door of the tomb Seven seals are placed on the stone, and a tent is set up close at hand for the use of the watch. On the Sabbath morning the sealed stone is inspected by a crowd of visitors from Jerusalem and the suburbs

(*o*) The next night, while two of the watch are on guard, a great voice is heard in heaven , the heavens are opened and two young men descend, clothed in light, and approach the tomb. The stone moves aside, and the two enter Presently the centurion and the Jewish elders, who have been awakened by the watch, see three men of supernatural height issue from the tomb ; one of the three, whose head reaches above the heavens, being supported or led by the other two. The three are followed by a Cross, and from it comes an answer of assent to a second voice from heaven which says, *Thou didst preach to them that sleep.* The second voice is succeeded by a second opening of the heavens, and another human form descends and enters the tomb.

(*p*) The Jews upon this hasten to Pilate and confess, *Truly this was the Son of God* Pilate retorts, *I am clean . the sentence was yours* At the earnest desire of the Jews he binds the watch to secrecy.

(*q*) The women, hitherto prevented by fear of the Jews, hasten at daybreak on Sunday to offer their last tribute at the tomb Their conversation on the way is reported at some length On arriving and finding the door open, they see a young man sitting in the middle of the tomb who says, *He is gone to the place from whence He was sent*

(*r*) The last day of the Feast having arrived, many are returning home, and among them the Twelve, who are still mourning for the Lord. Simon Peter and Andrew take their nets and go to the Sea, accompanied by Levi.

It is evident that the new incidents recited above rest upon the basis of a story which is in the main identical with that of the canonical Gospels They presuppose (e g) the intervention of the Jewish leaders, of Herod, and of Pilate in the trial of the Lord, the Mockery, the Crucifixion, the Three Hours' Darkness, the Burial in the garden-tomb, the descent of Angels, the Resurrection (in whatever sense), the visit of the women to the tomb, the departure of certain of the disciples to Galilee A careful study will shew that even details which seem to be entirely new, or which directly contradict the canonical narrative, may have been suggested by it, see e g (*c*), (*e*), (*g*), (*m*), (*q*) At other points we can detect the influence of the Old Testament ((*d*), (*h*), (*n*)), of New Testament books other than the Gospels ((*b*), (*l*), (*o*)), and of hymns or other liturgical forms ((*j*), (*o*)) It is worthy of especial remark that the fragment does not yield a single *agraphon*, for the saying in (*j*) is clearly based on the Fourth Word from the Cross Nor are there any certain indications of an independent tradition in the circumstantial treatment of the history Thus notwithstanding the large amount of new matter which it contains, there is nothing in this portion of the Petrine Gospel which compels us to assume the use of historical sources other than the canonical Gospels

2 The Petrine Passion-history on the other hand omits many important details which are related by one or more of the Four Gospels The following are the principal of these omissions , after each will be found a reference to the Evangelist or Evangelists to whom we owe our knowledge.

(*a*) The mockers do homage to the Lord, saying *Hail, King of the Jews* (Mt., Mk)

(*b*) The Lord goes forth bearing His Cross (J.).

(*c*) It is subsequently laid on Simon of Cyrene (Mt , Mk , L.).

(*d*)   The women follow with lamentations (L.).

(*e*)   The Crucifixion takes place at the third hour (Mk.)

(*f*)   The Lord refuses the first potion offered Him (Mt.,
Mk.)

(*g*)   The First Word from the Cross (L.).

(*h*)   Pilate refuses to change the superscription (J).

(*i*)   Lots are cast for the χιτών only (J).

(*j*)   The Crucified is mocked by the passers by and the
Priests (Mt , Mk., L)   He is reviled at first by both the malefactors
(Mt , Mk).

(*k*)   The Second Word (L.)

(*l*)   The Third Word (J)

(*m*)   The cry *Eli* is mistaken for a call for Elias (Mt , Mk).

(*n*)   A sponge full of vinegar is put to the Lord's lips (Mt ,
Mk).

(*o*)   The Fifth Word (J.)

(*p*)   The Sixth Word (J.)

(*q*)   The Seventh Word (L.)

(*r*)   Many of the dead come forth from their graves (Mt).

(*s*)   The centurion at the Cross confesses the divinity (Mt ,
Mk) or the innocence (L) of the Sufferer.

(*t*)   The Lord's Side is pierced (J)

(*u*)   Nicodemus takes part in the Burial (J)

(*x*)   The women witness the Burial, and return to keep the
Sabbath (L , J).

(*y*)   An earthquake attends the descent of the Angel (Mt).

(*z*)   The Angel announces, *He goeth before you into Galilee*
(Mt., Mk)

(*a₁*)   The women carry tidings to the Apostles (Mt , L.)

(*b₁*)   The tomb is visited by St Peter (L), and St John (J.).

To this list of omissions should probably be added the appearances of the Risen Christ on Easter Day and on the first
Sunday after Easter.   But to deal with those which are beyond dis-
pute, it may be observed that of twenty-seven only three belong to
the common tradition of the Synoptists, whilst not a single circumstance which is related by both the Synoptists and St John has been
altogether ignored in the Petrine narrative.   On the other hand sixteen of the omissions occur in the case of details recorded by one
Evangelist only (J., 9 , L., 4 , Mt., 2 ; Mk., 1).

3 Let us next compare the five accounts with the view of discovering how much our fragment has in common with the canonical Gospels. The following are the common facts

(*a*) Pilate washes his hands (Mt)

(*b*) Herod participates in the trial of the Lord (L).

(*c*) The Lord is delivered over to the people (J)

(*d*) He is attired in purple, crowned with thorns, spat upon, buffeted (Mt , Mk., J).

(*e*) He is crucified between two malefactors (Mt , Mk , L , J.).

(*f*) He is silent (Mt , Mk , L., but under other circumstances).

(*g*) A superscription is placed on the Cross (Mt , Mk , L , J).

(*h*) The Lord's garments are divided (Mt., Mk , L , J)

(*i*) One of the malefactors acknowledges His innocence (L.).

(*j*) There is darkness from noon to 3 p m (Mt , Mk , L)

(*k*) A potion is administered to the Lord shortly before His death (Mt , Mk , J).

(*l*) The Fourth Word from the Cross (Mt , Mk)

(*m*) The veil of the Temple is rent (Mt., Mk , L).

(*n*) An earthquake follows the Lord's Death (Mt)

(*o*) He is buried by Joseph (Mt , Mk , L , J) in a garden (J).

(*p*) The spectators are seized with remorse (L).

(*q*) The Jewish leaders request Pilate to set a watch at the tomb (Mt)

(*r*) A great stone is rolled to the mouth of the tomb (Mt., Mk)

(*s*) Two Angels descend (L , J.).

(*t*) One Angel descends (Mt , Mk)

(*u*) Mary Magdalene and other women visit the tomb early on Easter Day, and learn from an Angel that He is risen (Mt., Mk., L.).

(*x*) Some of the Disciples depart to Galilee and return to their fishing ([Mt., Mk.], J.).

An analysis of this common matter will shew that of twenty-two points which the Petrine fragment shares with one or more of the canonical Gospels, four are to be found in all the Gospels, seven in three out of the four, three more are in both St Matthew and St Mark, three are in St Matthew only and three in St Luke only. Comparing these results with those obtained under the head of omissions (p xvi.), we gather that the Petrine narrative largely embodies the common matter of the canonical Gospels, agreeing with the Synoptists in eight particulars, and omitting only three which they all relate, and further, that it has distinct points of coincidence with the combined witness of the First and Second Gospels, and with the separate witness of the First Gospel and of the Third There are only two or three incidents in the fragment which directly suggest acquaintance with the narrative of the Fourth Gospel, although, as we shall presently see, there are isolated expressions which render such an acquaintance probable

4 We may now proceed to a verbal comparison

Does the new fragment betray such a dependence upon the words of the canonical Gospels as to justify the belief that they were before the Petrine writer? The writer, it is clear, is not a mere compiler or harmonist, usually he appears to avoid the precise words of the canonical narrative, and when he comes nearest to them, it is his habit to change the order of the events, or to break the sequence by the intrusion of phraseology foreign to the writers of the New Testament. His narrative is *ex hypothesi* original, for it is attributed to St Peter, and he could not consistently with this assumption have borrowed the exact words of any existing Gospel But this consideration adds weight to any verbal coincidences which may reveal themselves. Such coincidences exist, and the following deserve especial attention

(a) ἀπενίψατο τὰς χεῖρας (Mt)

ἐνίψατο τὰς χεῖρας (P).

(b) προσελθὼν τῷ Πειλάτῳ ᾐτήσατο τὸ σῶμα (Mt., L., cf. Mk.).

ἦλθεν πρὸς τὸν Πειλᾶτον καὶ ᾔτησε τὸ σῶμα (P.)

(c) τὸ καταπέτασμα τοῦ ναοῦ ἐσχίσθη εἰς δύο (Mt, Mk., cf L.)

διεράγη τὸ καταπέτασμα τοῦ ναοῦ . εἰς δύο (P)

(d) ἐνείλησεν τῇ σινδόνι (Mk)

εἴλησε σινδόνι (P.).

(e) πενθοῦσι καὶ κλαίουσιν ('Mk ')

πενθοῦντες καὶ κλαίοντες (P)

(f) συνήχθησαν οἱ ἀρχιερεῖς καὶ οἱ Φαρισαῖοι πρὸς Πειλᾶτον (Mt).

συναχθέντες δὲ οἱ γραμματεῖς καὶ Φαρισαῖοι καὶ πρεσβύτεροι πρὸς ἀλλήλους .ἦλθον πρὸς Πειλᾶτον (P.).

(g) μή ποτε ἐλθόντες οἱ μαθηταὶ αὐτοῦ κλέψωσιν αὐτόν (Mt).

μή ποτε ἐλθόντες οἱ μαθηταὶ αὐτοῦ κλέψωσιν αὐτόν (P.).

(h) τίς ἀποκυλίσει ἡμῖν τὸν λίθον ἐκ τῆς θύρας τοῦ μνημείου; ..ἦν γὰρ μέγας σφόδρα (Mk)

τίς δὲ ἀποκυλίσει ἡμῖν καὶ τὸν λίθον τὸν τεθέντα ἐπὶ τῆς θύρας τοῦ μνημείου; μέγας γὰρ ἦν ὁ λίθος (P.).

It can scarcely be doubtful that these coincidences imply the use of the First and Second Gospels, and the conclusion is confirmed by a host of minuter correspondences which will be found in the footnotes, that many of these are scattered through contexts otherwise widely at issue with the canonical texts, serves only to add strength to the conviction. In the case of the Third Gospel the parallels are not so complete, yet they are sufficiently close to create a strong presumption in favour of its use, compare e.g.

(*a*) σάββατον ἐπέφωσκεν (L) σάββατον ἐπιφώσκει (P)

(*b*) ἤγοντο δὲ καὶ ἕτεροι κακοῦργοι καὶ ἤνεγκον δύο κακούργους (P.).
δύο (L).

(*c*) εἷς δὲ τῶν κρεμασθέντων κακούρ- εἷς δέ τις τῶν κακούργων ἐκείνων
γων (L) (P)

(*d*) Woe to us . because of our οὐαὶ ταῖς ἁμαρτίαις ἡμῶν (P.)
sins (L., Syr^{curet})

(*e*) πάντες οἱ ὄχλοι τύπτοντες τὰ ὁ λαὸς ἅπας . κόπτεται τὰ στήθη
στήθη ὑπέστρεφον (L.) (P)

(*f*) ὄντως ὁ ἄνθρωπος οὗτος δίκαιος ἴδετε ὅτι πόσον δίκαιός ἐστιν (P).
ἦν (L.).

(*g*) τῇ δὲ μιᾷ τοῦ σαββάτου ὄρθρου ὄρθρου δὲ τῆς κυριακῆς ἦλθε ἐπὶ
βαθέως ἐπὶ τὸ μνῆμα ἦλθαν τὸ μνημεῖον (P.).
(L).

Let us next compare the Petrine fragment with the Fourth Gospel. Here the traces of verbal indebtedness are fainter, yet the following occur

(*a*) παρέδωκεν αὐτὸν αὐτοῖς (J). παρέδωκεν αὐτὸν τῷ λαῷ (P.).

(*b*) ἡ ἑορτὴ τῶν Ἰουδαίων (J.) τῆς ἑορτῆς αὐτῶν (P).

(*c*) οὐκ εἶχες ἐξουσίαν κατ᾽ ἐμοῦ (J) ἐξουσίαν αὐτοῦ ἐσχηκότες (P.).

(*d*) ἐκάθισεν ἐπὶ βήματος (J). ἐκάθισεν αὐτὸν ἐπὶ καθέδραν κρίσεως (P.)

(*e*) ἐμαστίγωσεν (J.). ἐμάστιζον (P.)

(*f*) λάχωμεν περὶ αὐτοῦ (J.) λαχμὸν ἔβαλον ἐπ᾽ αὐτοῖς (P.).

(*g*) κατέαξαν τὰ σκέλη (J.). ἵνα μὴ σκελοκοπηθῇ (P.).

(*h*) ἵνα τελειωθῇ ἡ γραφή τετέ- ἐπλήρωσαν πάντα, καὶ ἐτελείω-
λεσται. ἵνα ἡ γραφὴ πλη- σαν   (P.).
ρωθῇ (J.).

(*i*) ἐν ταῖς χερσὶν αὐτοῦ τὸν τύπον ἀπέσπασαν τοὺς ἥλους ἀπὸ τῶν
τῶν ἥλων (J.). χειρῶν (P.).

(*j*) ἦν δὲ ἐν τῷ τόπῳ ὅπου ἐσταυρώθη τάφον καλούμενον Κῆπον Ἰωσήφ
κῆπος καὶ ἐν τῷ κήπῳ μνημεῖον (J) (P)

(*k*) ὁ κόσμος χαρήσεται (J).   ἐχάρησαν οἱ Ἰουδαῖοι (P)
(*l*) ἐπέχρισέν μου τοὺς ὀφθαλμούς(J)   ἐπέχρισαν ἑπτὰ σφραγῖδας (P)
(*m*) διὰ τὸν φόβον τῶν Ἰουδαίων (J.).   φοβουμένη διὰ τοὺς Ἰουδαίους(P.)
(*n*) τίνα ζητεῖς, (J)   τίνα ζητεῖτε, (P.).
(*o*) παρακύψας βλέπει (J.).   παρέκυψαν παρακύψατε (P.)
(*p*) εἰς τῶν δώδεκα (J)   οἱ δώδεκα (P.).
(*q*) ἐπορεύθησαν ἕκαστος εἰς τὸν οἶκον ἕκαστος ἀπηλλάγη εἰς τὸν οἶκον
     αὐτοῦ ('J.').   αὐτοῦ (P).
(*r*) ἐπὶ τῆς θαλάσσης (J.).   εἰς τὴν θάλασσαν (P).

If none of these parallels is by itself convincing, yet their cumulative force is considerable It may be admitted that the Petrine writer does not shew as much familiarity with the Fourth Gospel as with the Second, or even with the Third, or perhaps it would be more exact to say that he has for whatever reason availed himself more freely of the Synoptic Gospels than of St John But that he had access to St John is at least probable, not merely on the ground of the verbal resemblances, but because at several points the Petrine story presupposes the Johannine order or characteristic features of the Johannine narrative Thus in Peter as in St John the events at the Cross begin in this order: (1) the crucifixion between the two malefactors, (2) the setting up of the title, (3) the parting of the clothes, the relative order in Mt, Mk, being (3) (2) (1), and in L., (1) (3) (2) (Lods, p. 20). Still more remarkable is Peter's adoption of St John's view as to the relation of the Passion to the first day of Unleavened Bread Lastly, the references in Peter to the burial of the Crucified before the Sabbath, the *Crurifragium*, the garden-tomb, the fear of the Jews which seized the disciples after the Passion, and the departure of some of the disciples to the Sea of Galilee for the purpose of fishing, may most naturally be regarded as depending upon statements by St John, which they distort or contradict.

Our investigation has thus far established a strong probability that in one form or another the canonical Gospels were known to the Petrine writer, a probability which approaches to a certainty in the case of the Second Gospel, possibly also of the First and of the Third, and which even in the case of the Fourth Gospel is sufficient to justify assent.

III.

But assuming this use of the Gospels, it is still open to consideration whether they were employed as separate documents or in a harmonised form. In order to get an answer to the question, let us in the first place see whether all the points which the Petrine fragment has in common with one or more of the canonical Gospels are to be found in the only second century Harmony that has survived If we take the points as they have been already enumerated (p. xvii.), and compare them with the Arabic version of Tatian's Diatessaron, the results may be tabulated as follows :

(*a*)   In T. (after *d*).

(*b*)   In T.

(*c*)   In T. (after *a*).

(*d*)   In T.

(*e*)   In T. from L.

(*f*)   In T. from Mt.

(*g*)   In T. from J.

(*h*)   In T from J. (after *q*).

(*i*)   In T.

(*j*)   In T. from Mt , L.

(*k*)   In T from Mt , Mk., J. (after *l*).

(*l*)   In T. from Mk.

(*m*)   In T. from Mt.

(*n*)   In T

(*o*)   In T. from L., J , L., Mk , Mt., Mk., J.

(*p*)   In T (before *o*).

(*q*)   In T.

(*r*)   In T. from Mt.

(*s*)   In T from L , J. (after *t* and *u*).

(*t*)   In T. from Mt., L , Mk., Mt

(*u*)   In T from Mt.

(*x*)   In T from [Mt., Mk.,] J

Thus it appears that the Diatessaron, as represented in the Arabic, although it does not exhaust the canonical materials, might have furnished the writer of our fragment with all the incidents which he shares with any of the Four Gospels. The order in Peter is not always the same as it seems to have been in Tatian, but differences of order may be disregarded in our enquiry, since they are equally embarrassing if we assume that the writer had recourse to the Gospels as separate books.

We may next proceed to compare the Diatessaron with our fragment more minutely, with the view of ascertaining whether Tatian would have provided the Petrine writer with the *words* which he seems to have adopted from the Four Gospels. We will place side by side with the Petrine narrative in certain crucial passages the corresponding portions of the Diatessaron, approximately represented in Greek[1]. I select the accounts of the Mockery, the Three Hours, the Burial, and the Visit of the women to the Tomb.

A. THE MOCKERY.

TATIAN

καὶ ἱμάτιον πορφυροῦν περιέβαλον αὐτόν, καὶ πλέξαντες στέφανον ἐξ ἀκανθῶν (*infra*, τὸν ἀκάνθινον στέφανον) ἐπέθηκαν αὐτοῦ τῇ κεφαλῇ (J)[2], καὶ κάλαμον ἐν τῇ δεξιᾷ αὐτοῦ ..καὶ ἐμπτύσαντες εἰς τὸ πρόσωπον αὐτοῦ (xxvi 67)[3] ἔλαβον τὸν κάλαμον καὶ ἔτυπτον εἰς τὴν κεφαλὴν αὐτοῦ (Mt), καὶ ἐδίδοσαν αὐτῷ ῥαπίσματα (J).

PETER.

καὶ πορφύραν αὐτὸν περιέβαλλον καί τις αὐτῶν ἐνεγκὼν στέφανον ἀκάνθινον ἔθηκεν ἐπὶ τῆς κεφαλῆς τοῦ κυρίου· καὶ ἕτεροι ἑστῶτες ἐνέπτυον αὐτοῦ ταῖς ὄψεσι, καὶ ἄλλοι τὰς σιαγόνας αὐτοῦ ἐράπισαν· ἕτεροι καλάμῳ ἔνυσσον αὐτόν, καί τινες αὐτὸν ἐμάστιζον.

B. THE THREE HOURS.

TATIAN.

ἀπὸ δὲ ἕκτης ὥρας σκότος ἐγένετο ἐπὶ [*tenebrae occupaverunt*] πᾶσαν τὴν γῆν ἕως ὥρας ἐνάτης (Mt.), τοῦ ἡλίου ἐκλείποντος (L.). καὶ τῇ ἐνάτῃ ὥρᾳ ἐβόησεν ὁ Ἰησοῦς φωνῇ μεγάλῃ Ἠλεὶ ἠλεὶ [*Jaill, Jaill*][4], λαμὰ σαβαχθανεί· ὅ ἐστιν μεθερμηνευόμενον Ὁ θεός μου ὁ θεός μου, εἰς τί ἐγκατέλιπές με, (Mk) μετὰ τοῦτο εἰδὼς ὁ Ἰησοῦς ὅτι ἤδη πάντα

PETER.

ἦν δὲ μεσημβρία, καὶ σκότος κατέσχε πᾶσαν τὴν Ἰουδαίαν καὶ ἐθορυβοῦντο καὶ ἠγωνίων μή ποτε ὁ ἥλιος ἔδυ καί τις αὐτῶν εἶπεν Ποτίσατε αὐτὸν χολὴν μετὰ ὄξους [cf T., *supra*] καὶ ἐπλήρωσαν πάντα, καὶ ἐτελείωσαν καὶ ὁ κύριος ἀνεβόησε λέγων Ἡ δύναμίς μου, ἡ δύναμις, κατέλειψάς με καὶ αὐτῆς τῆς ὥρας διεράγη τὸ

---

[1] The plan adopted has been to substitute for Ciasca's translation of the Arabic Tatian the corresponding portions of the canonical Gospels The text has been determined by a comparison of Ciasca's Latin with Moesinger's *Evangelii Concordantis expositio* and the Curetonian Syriac of Luke xxiii , xxiv It claims of course only to be an approximate

and provisional representation of the text of the original work

[2] The order is that of Mt ; so in Ephraim (Moesinger, p. 239)

[3] So Ephraim in this context "et spuerunt in faciem eius" (p. 239)

[4] Ephraim "Eli Eli, quare me dereliquisti?"

τετέλεσται, ἵνα τελειωθῇ ἡ γραφὴ
λέγει Διψῶ ὅτε οὖν ἔλαβεν τὸ ὄξος
ὁ Ἰησοῦς εἶπεν Τετέλεσται [con-
summata sunt omnia] (J.) καὶ ἰδοὺ
τὸ καταπέτασμα τοῦ ναοῦ ἐσχίσθη
ἀπ' ἄνωθεν ἕως κάτω εἰς δύο, καὶ ἡ
γῆ ἐσείσθη ὁ δὲ ἑκατόνταρχος καὶ
οἱ μετ' αὐτοῦ ἐφοβήθησαν σφόδρα
(Mt.)[1].

καταπέτασμα τοῦ ναοῦ τῆς Ἱερου-
σαλὴμ εἰς δύο καὶ ἡ γῆ πᾶσα
ἐσείσθη καὶ φόβος μέγας ἐγένετο ..τότε ἥλιος ἔλαμψε καὶ εὑρέθη
ὥρα ἐνάτη

C. THE BURIAL.

TATIAN

Ἦλθεν ἀνὴρ ὀνόματι Ἰωσήφ,
πλούσιος καὶ βουλευτής (Mt , L.)
ὢν μαθητὴς τοῦ Ἰησοῦ (J) ..εἰσῆλθεν
πρὸς τὸν Πειλᾶτον καὶ ᾐτήσατο τὸ
σῶμα τοῦ Ἰησοῦ (Mk) ἐκέλευσεν
ἀποδοθῆναι (Mt). καὶ ἀγοράσας
σινδόνα καθελὼν αὐτὸν ἐνείλησεν
τῇ σινδόνι (Mk.) ἔλαβον οὖν τὸ
σῶμα τοῦ Ἰησοῦ ἦν δὲ ἐν τῷ τόπῳ
ὅπου ἐσταυρώθη κῆπος καὶ ἐν τῷ
κήπῳ μνημεῖον (J.) καὶ προσκυλί-
σαντες λίθον μέγαν τῇ θύρᾳ τοῦ μνημείου ἀπῆλθον (Mt)

PETER.

Ἰωσὴφ ὁ φίλος Πειλάτου καὶ τοῦ
κυρίου ἦλθεν πρὸς τὸν Πειλᾶτον
καὶ ᾔτησε τὸ σῶμα τοῦ κυρίου πρὸς
ταφήν. ..

δεδώκασι τῷ Ἰωσὴφ τὸ σῶμα
αὐτοῦ ἵνα αὐτὸ θάψῃ λαβὼν δὲ τὲν
κύριον ἔλουσε καὶ εἴλησε σινδόνι
καὶ εἰσήγαγεν εἰς ἴδιον τάφον καλούμενον Κῆπον Ἰωσήφ.
καὶ κυλίσαντες λίθον μέγαν
ὁμοῦ πάντες οἱ ὄντες ἐκεῖ ἔθηκαν
ἐπὶ τῇ θύρᾳ τοῦ μνήματος

D. THE VISIT OF THE WOMEN TO THE TOMB.

TATIAN

ὀψὲ δὲ σαββάτων τῇ ἐπιφω-
σκούσῃ εἰς μίαν σαββάτων (Mt),
ὄρθρου βαθέως (L), ἦλθεν Μαρία ἡ
Μαγδαληνὴ καὶ ἡ ἄλλη Μαρία καὶ
αἱ λοιπαί (L)[2], θεωρῆσαι τὸν
τάφον (Mt.), φέρουσαι ἃ ἡτοίμασαν
ἀρώματα (L) καὶ ἔλεγον πρὸς
ἑαυτὰς Τίς ἀποκυλίσει ἡμῖν τὸν λίθον

PETER.

τῇ δὲ νυκτὶ ᾗ ἐπέφωσκεν ἡ
κυριακή ὄρθρου τῆς κυριακῆς
Μαριὰμ ἡ Μαγδαληνὴ λαβοῦσα
μεθ' ἑαυτῆς τὰς φίλας ἦλθε ἐπὶ τὸ
μνημεῖον ὅπου ἦν τεθείς καὶ ἔλεγον
τίς δὲ ἀποκυλίσει ἡμῖν καὶ
τὸν λίθον τὸν τεθέντα ἐπὶ τῆς
θύρας τοῦ μνημείου; μέγας

---

[1] Ephraim (p. 257) "postea denuo
luxit."

[2] The Curetonian Syriac adds to Luke

xxiv. 1 "and there were with them other
women " Comp Tisch ad loc.

ἐκ τῆς θύρας τοῦ μνημείου, ἦν γὰρ
μέγας σφόδρα καὶ ἐλθοῦσαι [*et
uenientes*] εὗρον τὸν λίθον ἀποκεκυλισμένον...ἀπὸ τοῦ μνημείου..
εἰσελθοῦσαι δὲ (L)...εἶδον ἐκεῖ (?)
νεανίσκον καθήμενον ἐν τοῖς δεξιοῖς
περιβεβλημένον στολὴν λευκήν (Mk.),
καὶ ἐθαμβήθησαν . εἶπεν ταῖς γυναιξίν
Μὴ φοβεῖσθε ὑμεῖς, οἶδα γὰρ ὅτι
Ἰησοῦν τὸν ἐσταυρωμένον ζητεῖτε·
οὐκ ἔστιν ὧδε, ἠγέρθη γάρ .δεῦτε
ἴδετε τὸν τόπον ὅπου ἔκειτο (Mt.)
ἦλθεν ..εἰς τὸ μνημεῖον καὶ παρακύψας βλέπει Μαρία δὲ ..παρέκυψεν
εἰς τὸ μνημεῖον καὶ θεωρεῖ δύο ἀγγέλους ἐν λευκοῖς καθεζομένους .ὅπου
ἔκειτο τὸ σῶμα τοῦ Ἰησοῦ...λέγει
αὐτῇ Ἰησοῦς τίνα ζητεῖς; (J.).

γὰρ ἦν ὁ λίθος. βάλωμεν ἃ φέρομεν εἰς μνημοσύνην αὐτοῖ.
καὶ ἀπελθοῦσαι εὗρον τὸν
τάφον ἠνεῳγμένον· καὶ προσελθοῦσαι παρέκυψαν ἐκεῖ καὶ ὁρῶσιν
ἐκεῖ τινα νεανίσκον καθεζόμενον
μέσῳ τοῦ τάφου, ὡραῖον καὶ περιβεβλημένον στολὴν λαμπροτάτην,
ὅστις ἔφη αὐταῖς Τί ἤλθατε; τίνα
ζητεῖτε; μὴ τὸν σταυρωθέντα
ἐκεῖνον; ἀνέστη καὶ ἀπῆλθεν· εἰ δὲ
μὴ πιστεύετε, παρακύψατε καὶ
ἴδατε τὸν τόπον ἔνθα ἔκειτο, ὅτι
οὐκ ἔστιν· ἀνέστη γάρ. τότε αἱ
γυναῖκες φοβηθεῖσαι ἔφυγον

This comparison does not justify the conclusion that the writer of
our fragment was limited to the use of the Diatessaron In B and C he
might have derived his knowledge of the canonical Gospels from this
source exclusively , in A and D, on the other hand, there are traces of
the influence of passages of St Mark which are not incorporated in the
Arabic Harmony. Thus in A, St Mark alone has πορφύραν, ἐνέπτυον,
and (in this immediate context) ἀκάνθινον στέφανον, yet only the initial
words of St Mark's account appear in the existing Harmony. In D,
again, the Arabic Tatian omits the clause καὶ ἐξελθοῦσαι ἔφυγον (Mark
xvi. 8), which is distinctly reflected by the closing words in the Petrine
account It is of course possible that in both cases the original Diatessaron contained the omitted passages, so that it would be unsafe to
draw any negative inference from these exceptions Still they must be
allowed due weight as detracting from the completeness of the case in
favour of Peter's indebtedness to Tatian. On the whole we may perhaps claim to have established a strong presumption that the Petrine
writer employed a harmony which in its general selection of extracts,
and in some of its minuter arrangements, very nearly resembled the
Harmony of Tatian This is not equivalent to saying that he used
Tatian, because there is some reason to think that there may have been
a harmony or harmonies earlier than Tatian , nor does it preclude the
use by Peter of one or more of the Gospels separately, in addition to

his use of a harmonised narrative   Nor again are we justified in extending this presumption beyond the limits of the narrative of the Passion, for the evidence derived from the fragment carries us no further   It is conceivable that the harmony to which our writer had access was a harmony of the Passion-history and not of the whole cycle of evangelical teaching.   The rest of his narrative might, if recovered, be found to present quite another set of phaenomena.   Thus the relation of the Petrine writer to Tatian remains for the present an open question , but enough has been said to render such a relation probable if further enquiries should lead us to place the Gospel of Peter after the publication of the Diatessaron.   The harmonising tendency of Peter seems to be sufficiently established.

IV.

In his chronology of the Passion-history the Petrine writer follows close in the steps of St John.   The Condemnation takes place on the day before the Sabbath (i e. the weekly Sabbath, since it is followed immediately by the Lord's Day) , and the Sabbath next after the Crucifixion coincides with the first day of Unleavened Bread.   The Crucifixion, therefore, occurred on Friday, Nisan 14, before the Passover began.

So far all is plain.   But there are two minor points which present considerable difficulty.

1.   After the Crucifixion the disciples are represented as keeping fast νυκτὸς καὶ ἡμέρας ἕως τοῦ σαββάτου (c. vii.).   Since the Paschal Sabbath began three hours after the Death of the Lord, it has been thought that Peter refers to the Sabbath of the following week, and this view is strengthened by the statement at the end of the fragment, that on the last day of the feast the disciples were still mourning   But it is more natural to interpret ἕως τοῦ σαββάτου in reference to the Paschal Sabbath, which is certainly intended in the context (c. viii.)   Yet if the Paschal Sabbath was the further limit of the fast, when did it begin?   Doubtless with the end of the Last Supper, i.e. according to the usual reckoning, on Thursday night.   But the *Didascalia*, which possibly represents the Petrine chronology in this matter, allows a longer interval, for it supposes the Passover to have been actually kept on Tuesday, Nisan 11[1] and the arrest to have followed

---

[1] v. 14, 17 τρεῖς ἡμέρας πρὸ τοῦ καιροῦ ἐποίησαν τὸ πάσχα, ἐνδεκάτῃ τοῦ μηνὸς τρίτῃ σαββάτων

the same evening The explanation would be satisfactory if it agreed with the data in c. II, but it can hardly be maintained in face of Peter's identification of the first day of unleavened bread with the Sabbath M. Lods thinks that Peter has transferred to the Gospel history the conditions of the Christian Paschal fast, but to make good his position he finds it necessary to translate ἕως τοῦ σαββάτου "until the end of the Sabbath" It is possible that we ought to understand νυκτὸς καὶ ἡμέρας as referring to the conventional treatment of the Darkness as an actual night, which allows for an interval of two nights and two days between the Last Supper and the beginning of the Sabbath But the true solution may be yet to seek.

2 What is ἡ τελευταία ἡμέρα τῶν ἀζύμων? M Lods, believing that Peter is still moving amongst Christian ideas, understands him to refer to Sunday, Nisan 16 (Easter Day). But is it conceivable that a writer who had correctly spoken of Nisan 15 as the first day of the feast, would have permitted himself to speak of Nisan 16 as the last? It is clearly his intention to follow the Jewish reckoning, and if so, "the last day of unleavened bread" can scarcely be any other than Friday, Nisan 21. Consequently he must be understood to pass over without notice the intervening period between the early morning of Easter Day, and the Friday after Easter, and to connect the return of the Disciples to Galilee with the latter day The effect is to eliminate all the appearances to the Women and to the Disciples on Easter Day, and the appearance to the Eleven on the Sunday after Easter. When the fragment breaks off we seem to be on the point of reaching the first revelation (according to Peter) of the Risen Lord to the mourning Apostles[1]. The last words appear to be moulded upon John xxi. 1, and it may be presumed that they introduced a scene more or less nearly corresponding to that which St John proceeds to describe

V.

The Petrine Gospel contains no verbal quotation from the Old Testament. One passage which appears to make a formal reference to Deuteronomy, gives merely the general sense of the passage, the Petrine version of the Fourth Word from the Cross is as far from the exact words of the Psalm as it is from those of the canonical Gospels. Perhaps the writer has been led by his anti-Judaic spirit to affect indifference to the Jewish Scriptures, there is significance in the phrase γέγραπται αὐτοῖς with which his only direct appeal to them is intro-

---

[1] The fast had been broken by the Sabbath; the mourning at least was resumed.

duced Nevertheless he has not been able to escape from the influence of the Psalms and the Prophets, his very opposition to Judaism has familiarised him with the testimonies which Christians of the second century were in the habit of citing in their controversies with the Jews. Several of his allusions are obscure and do not carry conviction at first sight, but can be recognised with little hesitation when they are compared with the direct quotations which are to be found in other writers. The following table may assist the student in making the comparison, he will doubtless be able to add to the list of patristic references, which makes no claim to completeness.

Deut. xxi. 23 (Josh. x. 37).	*Ev. Pet.* i. iv	Just. *dial* 89. Tert *Iud.* 10. Epiph. *haer.* 66, 80.
Ps. ii. 1, 2.	*Ev. Pet.* i ii.	Tert. *res. carn.* 20, *Prax.* 28. *Const. Ap.* v 19
Ps. xxi. (xxii.) 1.	*Ev. Pet* iv.	Just. *dial* 99. Eus. *dem. ev* x 8.
Ps. xxi. (xxii.) 19.	*Ev. Pet.* iv.	Barn. 6. 7. Just. *dial.* 97, *apol.* 1. 38. Tert. *Iud.* 10. *Marc.* iv. 42. *Const. Ap.* v. 14. Cyril. H *catech.* xiii 26.
Ps. lxviii. (lxix) 22.	*Ev. Pet* v.	Barn. 7. 3—5 Sibyll. viii. 303. *Const. Ap.* v 14. Tert. *Iud.* 10. *Marc.* iv. 42 Cyril. H *catech.* xiii. 29.
Ps. lxxiii (lxxiv.) 4, 5.	*Ev. Pet.* iii.	*Const. Ap* v 15.
Isa. l. 6.	*Ev. Pet.* iii.	Barn. 5. 14.
Isa. lviii. 2 (cf. Ps. lxxi 1, 2, &c.).	*Ev. Pet.* iii	Just. *apol* 1 35.
Hosea x. 6.	*Ev. Pet.* i.	Just. *dial.* 103. Cyril H. *catech.* xiii. 14.
Amos viii. 9, 10.	*Ev. Pet.* v. viii.	Iren. iv 33. 12. Tert *Iud.* 10. *Marc.* iv. 42. Eus. *dem. ev.* x. 6.
Zech. xi. 13, Aq. (cf. Matt. xxvi. 9).	*Ev. Pet* iii.	Tert *Marc.* iv. 40. Cyril. H. *catech.* xiii. 10
Zech. xiv. 6, 7.	*Ev. Pet.* v.	*Const. Ap.* v. 14. Eus. *dem. ev.* x. 7. Cyril. H. *catech.* xiii. 24.

In the absence of formal quotations it is precarious to speculate upon the writer's use of a version His references to Pss xxii 19, lxix. 22, lxxiv. 4, 5, Amos viii. 9, 10, seem to involve the use of a version and, in Ps. lxxiv at least, of the LXX. Two or three very unusual words may suggest acquaintance with Symmachus On the other hand, his rendering of the Fourth Word implies a knowledge of the original, unless he has borrowed it from a secondary source.

VI

We proceed to enquire whether there are any signs of a tacit use by early Church-writers of the Petrine narrative of the Passion Traces of such use have already been sought with some success in various directions. The reader will find below a comparative view of the supposed allusions to Peter which have come to light in writings of the second third and fourth centuries.

GOSPEL OF ST PETER.	EPISTLE OF BARNABAS[1].
καί τις αὐτῶν εἶπεν Ποτίσατε αὐτὸν χολὴν μετὰ ὄξους, καὶ κεράσαντες ἐπότισαν (c v).	ἀλλὰ καὶ σταυρωθεὶς ἐποτίζετο ὄξει καὶ χολῇ. ἀκούσατε πῶς περὶ τούτου πεφανέρωκαν οἱ ἱερεῖς τοῦ ναοῦ τί οὖν λέγει ἐν τῷ προφήτῃ; Καὶ φαγέτωσαν ἐκ τοῦ τράγου τοῦ προσφερομένου τῇ νηστείᾳ ὑπὲρ πασῶν τῶν ἁμαρτιῶν. προσέχετε ἀκριβῶς Καὶ φαγέτωσαν οἱ ἱερεῖς μόνοι πάντες τὸ ἔντερον ἄπλυτον μετὰ ὄξους πρὸς τί; ἐπειδὴ ἐμὲ ὑπὲρ ἁμαρτιῶν μέλλοντα τοῦ λαοῦ μου τοῦ καινοῦ προσφέρειν τὴν σάρκα μου, μέλλετε ποτίζειν χολὴν μετὰ
ἐπὶ δε τούτοις πᾶσιν ἐνηστεύομεν... ὁ λαὸς ἅπας. κόπτεται τὰ στήθη (c. vii. viii).	ὄξους, φάγετε ὑμεῖς μόνοι, τοῦ λαοῦ νηστεύοντος καὶ κοπτομένου (7. 3—5).

GOSPEL OF ST PETER

ἐνέπτυον ἐράπισαν ἐμάστιζον
(c. iii).

αὐτὸς δὲ ἐσιώπα (c. iv.)

στέφανον ἀκάνθινον (c III).

καλάμῳ ἔνυσσον αὐτόν (c. III.).

νομίζοντες ὅτι νύξ ἐστιν (c. v).

ἐκήρυξας τοῖς κοιμωμένοις (c. ix)

SIBYLLINE ORACLES.

δώσουσιν δὲ θεῷ ῥαπίσματα
χερσὶν ἀνάγνοις | καὶ στόμασιν μια-
ροῖς ἐμπτύσματα φαρμακόεντα. |
δώσει δ᾽ ἐς μάστιγας ἁπλῶς ἁγνὸν
τότε νῶτον, | καὶ κολαφιζόμενος σι-
γήσει, μή τις ἐπιγνῷ | τίς τίνος ἢ
πόθεν ἦλθεν, ἵνα φθιμένοισι λαλή-
σει. | καὶ στέφανον φορέσει τὸν
ἀκάνθινον | πλευρὰς νύξουσιν
καλάμῳ διὰ τὸν νόμον αὐτῶν |.
ἐς δὲ τὸ βρῶμα χολὴν καὶ πιέμεν
ὄξος ἔδωκαν | νὺξ ἔσται σκοτό-
εσσα πελώριος ἐν τρισὶν ὥραις |.
ἥξει δ᾽ εἰς Ἅιδην ἀγγέλλων ἐλ-
πίδα πᾶσιν | τοῖς ἁγίοις (viii. 288
sqq.).

GOSPEL OF ST PETER

τῶν δὲ Ἰουδαίων οὐδεὶς .. οὐδὲ
Ἡρῴδης. ἀνέστη Πειλᾶτος (c. i.).

ἔλεγον Σύρωμεν τὸν υἱὸν τοῦ θεοῦ
καὶ ἐκάθισαν αὐτὸν ἐπὶ καθέδραν
κρίσεως, λέγοντες Δικαίως κρῖνε, βασιλεῦ τοῦ Ἰσραήλ (c. III.)
καὶ τεθεικότες τὰ ἐνδύματα ἔμπροσθεν αὐτοῦ διεμερίσαντο, καὶ λαχμὸν ἔβαλον ἐπ᾽ αὐτοῖς (c. IV.)

JUSTIN MARTYR[1]

μηνύει [τὸ προφητικὸν πνεῦμα]
τὴν γεγενημένην Ἡρῴδου τοῦ βα-
σιλέως Ἰουδαίων καὶ αὐτῶν Ἰουδαίων καὶ Πιλάτου τοῦ ὑμετέρου παρ᾽
αὐτοῖς γενομένου ἐπιτρόπου κατὰ
τοῦ Χριστοῦ συνέλευσιν (apol. 1 40).
καὶ γὰρ (ὡς εἶπεν ὁ προφήτης)
διασύροντες αὐτὸν ἐκάθισαν ἐπὶ
βήματος καὶ εἶπον Κρῖνον ἡμῖν
(apol 1 35)
Δαβὶδ εἶπεν ἐν εἰκοστῷ πρώτῳ
ψαλμῷ Διεμερίσαντο τὰ ἱμάτιά μου
ἑαυτοῖς καὶ ἐπὶ τὸν ἱματισμόν μου
ἔβαλον κλῆρον οἱ σταυρώσαντες αὐτὸν ἐμέρισαν τὰ ἱμάτια αὐτοῦ ἑαυτοῖς,
λαχμὸν βάλλοντες ἕκαστος κατὰ
τὴν τοῦ κλήρου ἐπιβολήν, ὃ ἐκλέξασθαι ἐβεβούλητο (dial. 97).

[1] The parallels between Justin and
Peter have been more fully worked out
by Harnack, pp 37—40, compare Zahn,
pp 66—70.

GOSPEL OF ST PETER.

τῶν δὲ Ἰουδαίων οὐδεὶς ἐνίψατο τὰς χεῖρας κ.τ.λ (c. i.).

καὶ τότε κελεύει Ἡρῴδης ὁ βασιλεὺς παραλημφθῆναι τὸν κύριον (c i.).

ἡμεῖς αὐτὸν ἐθάπτομεν γέγραπται γὰρ .ἥλιον μὴ δῦναι ἐπὶ πεφονευμένῳ (c. 1.).

παρέδωκεν αὐτὸν τῷ λαῷ πρὸ μιᾶς τῶν ἀζύμων, τῆς ἑορτῆς αὐτῶν (c. 11.).

νομίζοντες ὅτι νύξ ἐστιν τότε ἥλιος ἔλαμψε, καὶ εὑρέθη ὥρα ἐνάτη (c. v.).

ἐνηστεύομεν, καὶ ἐκαθεζόμεθα. νυκτὸς καὶ ἡμέρας ἕως τοῦ σαββάτου (c. vii.).

GOSPEL OF ST PETER.

τῶν δὲ Ἰουδαίων οὐδεὶς ἐνίψατο τὰς χεῖρας καὶ μὴ βουληθέντων νίψασθαι (c 1.).

αὐτὸς δὲ ἐσιώπα ὡς μηδὲν πόνον ἔχων (c iv).

σκότος κατέσχε πᾶσαν τὴν Ἰουδαίαν (c. v.).

καί τις αὐτῶν εἶπεν Ποτίσατε αὐτὸν χολὴν μετὰ ὄξους· καὶ κερά-

DIDASCALIA[1] AND APOSTOLICAL CONSTITUTIONS

ὁ μὲν ἀλλόφυλος κριτὴς νιψάμενος τὰς χεῖρας εἶπεν Ἀθῷός εἰμι ὁ δὲ Ἰσραὴλ ἐπεβόησε Τὸ αἷμα αὐτοῦ ἐφ' ἡμᾶς (v. 19).

καὶ Ἡρῴδης ὁ βασιλεὺς ἐκέλευσεν αὐτὸν σταυρωθῆναι (ib. cf. A. C).

Πιλᾶτος ὁ ἡγεμὼν καὶ ὁ βασιλεὺς Ἡρῴδης ἐκέλευσαν αὐτὸν σταυρωθῆναι (v. 19).

θάπτεται πρὸ ἡλίου δύσεως (A.C. v. 14)

ἐν αὐτῇ γὰρ ἐν μέσῳ αὐτῶν τῆς ἑορτῆς ἐσταύρωσάν με (v. 15)

ἔπειτα ἐγένετο τρεῖς ὥρας σκότος καὶ ἐλογίσθη νύξ, καὶ πάλιν ἀπὸ ἐνάτης ὥρας ἡμέρα (v. 14)

οὕτω γὰρ ἐνηστεύσαμεν καὶ ἡμεῖς παθόντος τοῦ κυρίου (v 19)

ORIGEN, hom. in Matt.[2]

[Pilatus] ipse quidem se lauit, illi autem se mundare noluerunt a sanguine Christi (§ 124).

in his omnibus [sc. spinis, calamo, delusione] unigenita illa uirtus nocita non est, sicut nec passa est aliquid (§ 125).

tenebrae tantum modo super omnem terram Iudaeam sunt factae ad horam nonam (§ 134).

sic [i.e. spongia impleta aceto] impleuit prophetiam in se dicentem

---

[1] The Didascalia has been quoted from Lagarde's retranslation printed in Bunsen's Anal. Ante-Nicaen ii

[2] See Mr J O. F. Murray's article Evangelium secundum Petrum in the Expositor for Jan 1893

σαντες ἐπότισαν καὶ ἐπλήρωσαν πάντα καὶ ἐτελείωσαν κατὰ τῆς κεφαλῆς αὐτῶν τὰ ἁμαρτήματα (c. v)

καὶ εἰπὼν ἀνελήφθη (c v.).

GOSPEL OF ST PETER.

τῶν δὲ Ἰουδαίων κ.τ.λ. (c. 1).

Ἡρῴδης ὁ βασιλεύς (c. 1).

καὶ τεθεικότες τὰ ἐνδύματα ἔμπροσθεν αὐτοῦ διεμερίσαντο, καὶ λαχμὸν ἔβαλον ἐπ᾽ αὐτοῖς (c. iv)

ἠγωνίων μή ποτε ὁ ἥλιος ἔδυ νομίζοντες ὅτι νύξ ἐστιν· τότε ἥλιος ἔλαμψε καὶ εὑρέθη ὥρα ἐνάτη (c v).

καί τις αὐτῶν εἶπεν Ποτίσατε αὐτὸν χολὴν μετὰ ὄξους· καὶ κεράσαντες ἐπότισαν (c v.)

[1] Mr Murray points out that Origen, like the writer of Peter, regards the χολή as noxious (*Matt* 1 37), and the *crurifragium* as an act of mercy (*ib* 140)
[2] The allusions in Cyril were first noticed (*Academy*, Dec 24, 1892) by Dr J H. Bernard, of Trinity College, Dublin, some further parallels have been pointed out to me by Mr A. E Brooke.

de se *Et dederunt in escam meam fel, et in siti mea potauerunt me aceto* ideo et secundum Ioannem cum accepisset Iesus acetum cum felle dixit *Consummatum est* (§ 137)[1]. statim ut clamauit ad Patrem receptus est post tres horas receptus est (§ 140).

CYRIL OF JERUSALEM, *catech.* xiii.[2]

ὁ μὲν γὰρ Πιλᾶτος ὕδατι ἀπενίπτετο τὰς χεῖρας· οἱ δὲ ἐπιβοῶντες ἔλεγον Τὸ αἷμα αὐτοῦ ἐφ᾽ ἡμᾶς (§ 21) Ἡρῴδης δὲ ἦν τότε βασιλεύς (§ 14).

οἱ στρατιῶται διεμερίσαντο τὸ περιβόλαιον εἰς τέσσαρα σχισθέν, ὁ δὲ χιτὼν οὐκ ἐσχίσθη καὶ λαχμὸς περὶ τούτου γίνεται τοῖς στρατιώταις, καὶ τὸ μὲν μερίζονται, περὶ τούτου δὲ λαγχάνουσιν ἆρα καὶ τοῦτο γέγραπται; Διεμερίσαντο τὰ ἱμάτιά μου ἑαυτοῖς καὶ ἐπὶ τὸν ἱματισμόν μου ἔβαλον κλῆρον· κλῆρος δὲ ἦν ὁ λαχμός (§ 26) μεσέμβολον ἦν ἆρα τὸ σκότος, ὠνόμασε δὲ ὁ θεὸς τὸ σκότος νύκτα. διὰ τοῦτο οὔτε ἡμέρα ἦν οὔτε νύξ... ἀλλὰ μετὰ τὴν ἐνάτην ἔλαμψεν ὁ ἥλιος (§ 24).

διψῶντι τῷ κυρίῳ σπόγγῳ πλησθέντι καὶ περιτεθέντι καλάμῳ προσκομίζει τὸ ὄξος· καὶ ἔδωκαν εἰς τὸ

One or two may be due to the *Didascalia*, but on the whole it is hardly possible to doubt that Cyril freely used the Gospel of Peter to illustrate his lectures, although he warns his catechumens against the private reading of *apocrypha* (*catech* iv. 33, 36 καί μοι μηδὲν τῶν ἀποκρύφων ἀναγίνωσκε κ τ λ).

ἀπέσπασαν τοὺς ἥλους ἀπὸ τῶν χειρῶν τοῦ κυρίου (c. vi) τῶν ἀζύμων, τῆς ἑορτῆς αὐτῶν (c iii.) ἔλεγον [αἱ γυναῖκες] . κλαύσομεν καὶ κοψόμεθα (c. xi). ἐγὼ δὲ μετὰ τῶν ἑταίρων μου ἐλυπούμην .. καὶ ἐκρυβόμεθα (c. vii).

βρῶμά μου χολήν κ τ λ. ποίαν δὲ χολὴν ἔδωκαν, ἔδωκαν αὐτῷ, φησίν, ἐσμυρνισμένον οἶνον χολώδης δὲ καὶ κατάπικρος ἡ σμύρνα (§ 29). ἐξέτεινεν ἀνθρωπίνας χεῖρας καὶ προσεπάγησαν ἥλοις (§ 28). ἐν ἀζύμων γὰρ ἡμέρᾳ καὶ ἑορτῇ αἱ μὲν γυναῖκες αὐτῶν ἐκόπτοντο καὶ ἔκλαιον, ὠδυνῶντο δὲ ἀποκρυβέντες οἱ ἀπόστολοι (§ 25)[1]

Of the writers who thus appear to exhibit indications of acquaintance with our fragment Origen, the writer of the *Didascalia*, Eusebius, and Cyril are later than the period at which the Petrine Gospel is known to have been in circulation On the other hand Barnabas, Justin, probably also the Sibylline writer, are earlier, and it is obviously of importance to determine their relation to Peter

1   In Barnabas we find prominence given to two particulars which are also prominent in Peter, the potion of mingled gall and vinegar, and the fasting and mourning that followed the Crucifixion. The former rests on Ps lxix 21, but whereas in the Psalm the χολή is regarded as food, in Barnabas, as in Peter, it is administered as a potion (Barn., μέλλετε ποτίζειν χολὴν μετὰ ὄξους: Pet , ποτίσατε αὐτὸν χολὴν μετὰ ὄξους) St Matthew doubtless goes half way towards this new reading of the Psalm (ἔδωκαν αὐτῷ πιεῖν οἶνον [v l ὄξος] μετὰ χολῆς μεμιγμένον), and both Barnabas and Peter may have arrived at it in this way but it is more natural to suppose that one of the two later writers depends upon the other Now in Barnabas we can discover the reason of the special significance attached to the χολή, it connects itself in the author's mind with certain features in the ritual of the Two Goats In Barnabas[2] again we catch a glimpse of the notion which underlies the statement as to the Disciples' fast, the Death of the Lord has transformed the Feast of the Passover into the Fast of the Day of Atonement. Both ideas rest on the symbolism of the Jewish Law. Peter

---

[1] The last four sections of the same *Catechesis* seem to bristle with allusions to our fragment (§ 38 περὶ τοῦ χιτῶνος λαχόντες § 39 οἱ λαχόντες περὶ τῶν ἱματίων (where Cyril forgets the distinction he has so carefully drawn in § 26), τὸ καταπέτασμα τοῦ ναοῦ τὸ τότε

διερραγέν. § 40 ἔχεις δώδεκα ἀποστόλους τοῦ σταυροῦ μάρτυρας § 41 τοῦτο [sc ὁ σταυρός] μετὰ τοῦ Ἰησοῦ φαίνεσθαι μέλλει πάλιν ἐξ οὐρανοῦ προσκυνοῦντες τὸν ἀποσταλέντα κύριον καὶ τὸν ἀποστείλαντα πατέρα
[2] Barn. 7 4

adopts them without explanation, in Barnabas we can see them taking shape and can trace them to their source It seems to follow that Peter is later than Barnabas and possibly borrows from him. If the Epistle of Barnabas was a work of the first century or of the early years of the second, it may not improbably have come into the hands of the party from which the Petrine Gospel emanated. Their strongly anti-Judaic temper would have made it a welcome document.

2. The resemblances between our fragment and the Eighth Book of the Sibylline Oracles are for the most part superficial. The phrases δώσουσιν ῥαπίσματα, δώσει δ᾽ ἐς μάστιγας .νῶτον, point to Isaiah l. 6; κολαφιζόμενος σιγήσει is probably a reference to 1 Pet. ii. 19, 23, στέφανον τὸν ἀκάνθινον may be a reminiscence of St Mark or St John But πλευρὰς νύξουσιν καλάμῳ throws important light on the Petrine καλάμῳ ἔνυσσον αὐτόν It connects the latter with John xix. 34 λόγχῃ αὐτοῦ τὴν πλευρὰν ἔνυξεν, while the next words in the Sibyllist, διὰ τὸν νόμον αὐτῶν, seem to shew that he has also in view the treatment of the Azazel described in Barn. 7. 8¹ (Tert. *adv Iud.* 14). Here the Petrine form is clearly the later, for it is further from St John There is also some connexion between the Sibylline νὺξ ἔσται.. ἐν τρισὶν ὥραις and the Petrine νομίζοντες ὅτι νύξ ἐστιν, but it is impossible to determine in this instance on which side the debt lies.

3. The problem of Peter's relations to Justin is one of great interest, and of some difficulty In *Dial* 106 we read· καὶ τὸ εἰπεῖν μετωνομα-κέναι αὐτὸν Πέτρον ἕνα τῶν ἀποστόλων καὶ γεγράφθαι ἐν τοῖς ἀπομνη-μονεύμασιν αὐτοῦ γεγενημένον καὶ τοῦτο σημαντικὸν ἦν τοῦ αὐτὸν ἐκεῖνον εἶναι δι᾽ οὗ καὶ τὸ ἐπώνυμον Ἰακὼβ τῷ Ἰσραὴλ ἐπικληθέντι ἐδόθη. In this passage Justin recognises the existence of certain ἀπομνημονεύ-ματα Πέτρου, i.e of a Petrine Gospel But the 'Memoirs of Peter' may represent the second of the canonical Gospels, and in Mark iii 16 the fact to which Justin refers is duly recorded It is therefore unnecessary to conclude that Justin refers to an apocryphal Gospel, nor is it easy to believe that if the Docetic Gospel of St Peter had fallen into his hands he could have been deceived with regard to its true character. Dismissing this consideration, we proceed to the alleged use of our frag-ment in the first *Apology* and the *Dialogue* The first instance (p. xxix.) need not detain us, it has nothing in common with Peter which cannot be explained by the influence of Ps. ii. and Acts iv. But the second and third quotations require careful discussion In the second Justin relates a

¹ καὶ ἐμπτύσατε πάντες καὶ κατακεντή-σατε καὶ περίθετε τὸ ἔριον τὸ κόκκινον περὶ τὴν κεφαλὴν αὐτοῦ, καὶ οὕτως εἰς ἔρημον βληθήτω

remarkable incident which he shares with Peter, and there are moreover points of verbal agreement. But (1) the incident seems to rest on a misinterpretation of John xix. 13 which might have occurred to both writers independently, their way of stating it is certainly independent. (2) The words put into the mouth of the mockers differ, and seem to be based on different passages of the Old Testament; Justin expressly refers to Isaiah lviii. 2, Peter seems to have in view similar words in the Psalms and Proverbs. (3) Peter's σύρωμεν may certainly have suggested Justin's διασύροντες, yet the resemblance is in sound rather than in meaning, and it is more likely that διασύροντες was supplied by the Old Testament, διέσυρον was substituted by Aquila for ἐμυκτήριζον in Prov. 1 30, LXX., a passage where Wisdom is represented as mocked by fools If on the whole it is thought that one of the two writers had the other in view, the evidence seems to point to a use of Justin by Peter, in Justin the words of St John are given exactly, in Peter they are varied, Justin's account of the incident is brief, Peter's is more diffuse, after the manner of a writer who is working upon the lines of an earlier authority

We turn to the third parallel. The points are two: both Justin and Peter use the remarkable phrase λαχμὸν βάλλειν, and both use it, not exclusively in reference to the χιτών, as St John does, but of the ἱμάτια in general. Since the phrase is not known to occur in any other connexion, and its use in this connexion is limited, as far as we know, to Justin, Peter and Cyril, it seems certain that its origin is to be sought for either in the earliest of those writers, or in some source which lies behind them all. That it was borrowed by Justin from Peter is improbable, for the context in Justin shews no sign of Petrine influence, on the contrary Justin speaks in it of the piercing of the Lord's Hands and Feet, whereas in Peter, notwithstanding Ps. xxii 16, the nails are drawn forth only from the Hands. On the other hand it is not necessary to suppose that Peter was indebted for the phrase directly to Justin. It is difficult to understand why either writer should have gone out of his way to adopt so singular an expression if it had not been previously known to him through an earlier rendering of Ps. xxii. 18 Now St John with that verse in view uses λάχωμεν[1], and Symmachus in the Psalm itself rendered יַפִּילוּ גוֹרָל by ἐλάγχανον. Is it overbold to conjecture that in another version which followed the Hebrew more closely, the reading was ἔβαλλον or ἔβαλον λαχμόν? Even in the case

---

[1] In his paraphrase of John xix 24 Nonnus twice uses λαχμός, but not in the phrase λαχμὸν βάλλειν He seems to understand the game known as πλειστοβολίνδα, cf D Heinsii exerc ad loc

of Cyril it may be doubted whether a traditional rendering or paraphrase of the Psalm is not present to his mind rather than Peter's use of the passage. For he is completely at issue with Peter's identification of the διαμερισμός and the λαχμός, the first, he points out, refers to the ἱμάτια, the second only to the χιτών (τὰ μὲν μερίζονται περὶ τούτου δὲ λαγχάνουσιν) Yet he clings to the phrase, even though he finds it necessary to explain what it means (κλῆρος δὲ ἦν ὁ λαχμός) Is it probable that while rejecting the statement of the Petrine Gospel, he would have retained and explained a difficult phrase connected with it, unless the phrase had possessed some higher claim upon his consideration than its place in an *apocryphon* would supply? On the whole there is reason to suppose that although in this instance the connexion between Justin and Peter (and perhaps Cyril also) is a real one, it implies no more than a relation to a common source. In the present state of our knowledge, this explanation can only be conjectural. on the other hand it is sufficiently probable to make us pause before we assert that Justin has used the Petrine fragment

Thus there is at present no satisfactory proof that our fragment was used by any writer before the end of the second century. The sparing and unacknowledged use of it by writers of the third and fourth centuries is in harmony with all that we know as to the origin and early circulation of the Petrine Gospel Such allusions do not compel us to modify our belief as to the relatively narrow area of its influence. The facts are consistent with a very moderate circulation within the limits of Syria and Palestine Some striking coincidences appear in the Didascalia and in the Apostolical Constitutions, both probably of Syrian and Palestinian origin The references in Origen occur only in the homilies on St Matthew, which belong to the last stage of his literary career when Caesarea and not Alexandria was the centre of his work. If, as seems nearly certain, the Gospel was known to Cyril, he knew it merely as one of the apocryphal books current in Palestine, against which he warns his catechumens while he is not unwilling to borrow from them any details which seemed impressive or edifying. It is not improbable that patristic students may stumble upon other traces of the Petrine story of the Passion in Church writers connected by birth or other circumstances with Antioch, Caesarea or Jerusalem. Of a direct influence exerted by it upon Egyptian and Western writers there is at present no sufficient evidence[1].

---

[1] Nonnus presents some interesting parallels (J M C , *Scottish Guardian*, March 10 1893), and Mr F. P Badham (*Athenæum*, May 13) points out others in Lactantius , but as proofs of a direct use of Peter they are not convincing

VII.

It is natural to attempt a comparison of the Petrine fragment with other survivals of apocryphal Gospel-literature   Our materials are as yet far too imperfect to yield large results   yet there are a few points which can be clearly seen

(1) The Gospel of Peter belongs to a class of writings which claimed to preserve the personal narrative of one of the Apostles   Such compositions seem to have been characteristic of the Gnostic sects of the second century; the Gospel or Tradition of Matthias e g was current among the Basilidians, the Gospel of Philip is attributed by Epiphanius to a sect of Ophite Gnostics   The Docetae of Western Syria followed the fashion of the age in putting forth a Gospel of this type, which received the name of the Apostolic founder of the Church of Antioch.

(2)   The Petrine Gospel, to judge by the Akhmîm fragment, was a free harmony of the canonical Gospels, rather than an attempt to rewrite the history.   Not a single *agraphon* is found in the fragment. This circumstance may indeed be due to the writer's purpose of representing the Lord as silent during the Passion.   But the manner in which he has handled his facts suggests another explanation.   He is unwilling to go far beyond the lines of the canonical narrative ∕ He is prepared to shift, transpose, reset his materials, but not to invent important sayings for which there is no authority in the canonical tradition.   This cautious conservatism differentiates the Gospel of Peter from the Gospel according to the Egyptians and the Gospel of the Hebrews, which, so far as we know them, were largely independent of the Canon.

(3)   It is scarcely to be doubted that our Gospel was written with the purpose of promoting Docetic, perhaps also Encratite views There were many methods open to the writer.   He might have contented himself, as Basilides and Valentinus appear to have done, with supplementing the canonical Gospels by expositions which grafted upon them the interpretations of his sect   Or he might have interpolated the canonical history, or, like Marcion, have selected one of the Gospels and submitted it to revision.   He has not followed either of these precedents.   His method is to exhibit a manipulated harmony. In form, however, his work is not a harmony, but a personal statement, and this literary fiction leaves him free to take certain liberties with the documents before him.   He allows himself another in-

dulgence which no mere harmonist could have ventured to take. He omits large portions of the narrative which were unfavourable to his views. He adds here and there a suggestive remark, he gives to familiar words a new turn which favours a non-catholic interpretation. He introduces apocalyptic passages which extend the simpler narrative of the Gospels in the direction of Gnostic speculation Yet the whole is done with so much skill that the heretical tendency of the fragment has been stoutly denied If we understand his position aright, the writer of Peter belonged to a minority whose policy was conciliation, and his purpose was not so much to supply a Gospel for the use of a sect, as to propagate a Docetic Christology within the Church from which he had not yet parted company.

Thus the Gospel of Peter seems to have held an unique position among the Gospels of the second century. To this circumstance we may venture to attribute its limited circulation. Serapion checked its acceptance within the Church. Among Separatists it was not sufficiently aggressive to secure general support If a harmony of the canonical Gospels were desired, it could be found in the work of Tatian if a new Gospel, strongly flavoured with distinctive tenets, many such were at hand. The Petrine Gospel shared the fate which commonly attends a compromise, it failed to satisfy either party, and fell into neglect.

Thus our Gospel stands to some extent alone among the apocryphal Gospels of the second century. But it has marked affinities with other groups of apocryphal writings. Its Gnostic and apocalyptic tone is in full sympathy with the literature which bears the name of Leucius Charinus, and it is difficult to avoid the inference that we have before us a product of the school of writers from which the *Circuits of the Apostles* proceeded during the second half of the second century. It was obviously in the hands of the author of the *Didascalia*, and has influenced the *Apostolical Constitutions.* Lastly, there are traces of its use in the various forms of the Acts of Pilate, but especially in the form which seems to be the latest of all, the *Anaphora Pilati.* A connexion has been supposed to exist between the Petrine Gospel and the *Ascension of Isaiah*, but the coincidence is one of ideas only and does not extend to the literary form.

VIII.

The Gospel of Peter, Serapion tells us, not only emanated from the Docetic party (τῶν καταρξαμένων αὐτοῦ οὓς Δοκητὰς καλοῦμεν), but its general tendency was Docetic (τὰ γὰρ πλείονα φρονήματα ἐκείνων ἐστὶ τῆς διδασκαλίας) This tendency did not, however, largely interfere with its representation of the facts, but was chiefly shewn in unorthodox additions (τὰ μὲν πλείονα τοῦ ὀρθοῦ λόγου τινὰ δὲ προσδιεσταλμένα)

In the fragment which survives accretions of this character are few, but their purpose is sufficiently clear We may schedule them in the fragment, as Serapion did throughout the Gospel

(1) The Lord's freedom from pain at the moment of Crucifixion.

(2) His desertion by His 'Power' at the moment of Death.

(3) The representation of His Death as an ἀνάληψις

(4) The supernatural height of the Angels and especially of the Risen Christ.

(5) The personification of the Cross

To this list we ought perhaps to add the sealing of the stone with seven seals. If our view of the order of the events is correct, the omission of all the Easter-week appearances must be attributed to the same tendency

Two or three general remarks may be added (*a*) Our fragment is intensely anti-Judaic in tone, a chief purpose is clearly to throw the full responsibility of the Crucifixion upon the Jews and to intensify their guilt. (*b*) It betrays no sign of an Ebionitic view of the Person of Christ; on the other hand, it gives prominence to His supernatural and Divine character By those who speak of Him He is invariably called ὁ υἱὸς τοῦ θεοῦ. by the writer himself He is designated ὁ κύριος, even when the reference is to the Dead Christ. Of the Three who issue from the tomb, the Christ alone towers above the heaven (*c*) The teaching of the fragment with regard to the Lord's Death and Resurrection, while open to suspicion, is not absolutely inconsistent with Catholic language Origen, as the notes will shew, has apparently used or adopted ἀνελήμφθη in reference to the Death of the Lord: and the Petrine writer distinctly asserts a Resurrection (ἀνέστη)

We may now enter upon the question, To what form of Docetism does our fragment incline?

1. One of the earliest forms of second century Docetism is criticised in the letters of Serapion's great predecessor in the see of Antioch, St Ignatius. Bishop Lightfoot[1] has characterised the Docetism which is condemned by the Ignatian letters as (1) "thorough going," (2) "Judaic." (1) It denied the reality of the Passion, it was scandalised by the Cross.

[1] *S. Ignatius,* i. 373

Ignatius meets it by asserting that the Lord was truly born, was truly arraigned before Pontius Pilate, was truly crucified and truly died[1] (2) Lightfoot maintains that the Judaism which Ignatius attacks was only another side of the Docetic heresy. His argument is not perhaps absolutely convincing, but it establishes a probability that the Ignatian Docetae were disposed to Judaize. Certainly there is no trace in the references of Ignatius to these heretics of any antagonism to Judaism on their part, whilst on the other hand it is obvious that there were important points of contact between them and the Judaizers.

In the early part of the second century this cruder form of Docetism seems to have been widely prevalent in the Churches of Asia Minor. It is condemned more or less directly in the Ignatian letters to Tralles, Smyrna, Ephesus, Magnesia, and Philadelphia; the only genuine writings of Ignatius which are free from all allusion to it are the letter to the Romans, and the personal letter to Polycarp. Yet it is clearly not the δόκησις with which the Petrine writer is in sympathy. For (1) he does not suggest that the Trial and the Crucifixion were putative; on the contrary he emphasises both events, only reserving for the Lord an immunity from physical pain And (2) he is not merely free from any suspicion of Judaizing; he is, as we have seen, aggressively anti-Judaic.

2. At first sight we may be tempted to connect our writer with the school of Cerinthus or of Carpocrates According to Irenaeus, who is followed by Hippolytus, Cerinthus taught that, though Jesus suffered, died and rose again, the Christ was impassible and left Him before the Passion[2]. Carpocrates, it seems, spoke of a Power which was sent down by the Unbegotten God upon the soul of Jesus, and eventually ascended to its source[3] Ideas of the same general character are to be found in our fragment, but they appear there in a more guarded, a more complex, and probably a later form. Moreover, the Judaizing tendency of Cerinthus and the humanitarianism of both Cerinthus and Carpocrates exclude the supposition of any direct influence having been exercised by them upon 'Peter.' The early 'Ophite' system described by Irenaeus approaches nearer to Peter's view. According to that system Jesus was born of a Virgin by Divine operation, subsequently the Christ descended on Him, withdrawing before the Crucifixion, after the Crucifixion a Power was sent down upon the Crucified which restored Him to life in a psychic and spiritual

[1] *Magn.* 9. *Eph* 8 *Trall* 9   33
[2] Iren 1 26 2, iii. 11. 1 Hipp vii   [3] Iren 1 25 1. Hipp. vii. 32

Body, the Body of the Flesh being however left behind[1] But the Petrine doctrine differs from this in a material point, for it regards the higher nature of the Lord as remaining with Him on the Cross up to the moment of His Death, nor is there any trace in 'Peter' of the other features of the intricate gnosis with which the Ophite Christology was closely bound up.

3 The two great schools of Basilides and Valentinus claimed for their founders spiritual descent from the Apostles Peter and Paul respectively[2] Both leaders appear to have accepted in substance the Gospels now regarded as canonical, admitting the facts of the Gospel history, while putting an heretical construction upon them Of the Basilidians Hippolytus expressly states. γέγονε πάντα ὁμοίως κατ᾽ αὐτοὺς . ὡς ἐν τοῖς εὐαγγελίοις γέγραπται[3]. But Basilides gave an entirely new complexion to both the Crucifixion and the Resurrection. The purpose of the Passion was the διαίρεσις of the composite factors of the Lord's Person, which restored each element to its proper sphere The σωματικὸν μέρος suffered and returned to ἀμορφία, the psychic was restored to the Hebdomad, and so forth With these ideas the Petrine fragment has nothing in common

The sphere of Basilides' influence seems to have been nearly limited to Egypt. Valentinus was the centre of a larger movement We find him first in Egypt, then in Cyprus, and finally, between A D 138 and 160, at Rome His followers were divided into two schools, Eastern and Western, the 'Anatolic' and the 'Italic' The Valentinians, according to Hippolytus[4], recognised two Christs, the aeon who, together with the Holy Spirit, emanated from Νοῦς and ᾿Αλήθεια, and another who was the common product of the whole Pleroma. To the Son of Mary they attributed a psychic, or, as the Eastern Valentinians preferred to say, a pneumatic Body The fragments of Valentinian teaching excerpted by Clement and representing chiefly the Eastern school, are nearer in tone and general tendency to the Petrine fragment than any Gnostic utterances we have as yet encountered. The following may be taken as specimens ·

ὁ κύριος διὰ πολλὴν ταπεινοφροσύνην οὐχ ὡς ἄγγελος ὤφθη ἀλλ᾽ ὡς ἄνθρωπος.. αὐτὸς γὰρ καὶ ἄνω φῶς ἦν καὶ ἔστι· τὸ ἐπιφανὲν ἐν σαρκὶ καὶ

---

[1] Iren. i. 30. 12, 13.

[2] Clem. Alex. *Strom.* vii. 17 καθάπερ ὁ Βασιλείδης, κἂν Γλαυκίαν ἐπιγράφηται διδάσκαλον, ὡς αὐχοῦσιν αὐτοί, τὸν Πέτρου ἑρμηνέα· ὡσαύτως δὲ καὶ Οὐαλεντῖνον Θεοδάδι ἀκηκοέναι φέρουσιν, γνώριμος δ᾽ οὗτος

γεγόνει Παύλου. Can Glaucias have been the name of the supposed translator of the Petrine Gospel, i e. the assumed name of the author?

[3] Hipp vii. 27.

[4] Hipp vi. 35.

τὸ ἐνταῦθα ὀφθὲν οὐχ ὕστερον τοῦ ἄνω, οὐδὲ διεκέκοπτο ᾗ ἄνωθεν μετέστη δεῦρο ἀλλ᾽ ἦν τὸ πάντῃ ὂν καὶ παρὰ τῷ πατρὶ κἀνταῦθα· δύναμις γὰρ ἦν τοῦ πατρός (*exc Theod* § 4) ἀναστὰς ὁ κύριος εὐηγγελίσατο τοὺς δικαίους τοὺς ἐν τῇ καταπαύσει καὶ μετέστησεν αὐτοὺς καὶ μετέθηκεν (§ 18).

ὁ σταυρὸς τοῦ ἐν πληρώματι ὅρου σημεῖόν ἐστιν χωρίζει γὰρ τοὺς ἀπίστους τῶν ἀπίστων, ὡς ἐκεῖνος τὸν κόσμον τοῦ πληρώματος (§ 42).

ὅτι μὲν οὖν αὐτὸς ἕτερος ἦν ᾧ ἀνείληφεν δῆλον ἐξ ὧν ὁμολογεῖ Ἐγὼ ἡ ζωή. καὶ ὅταν λέγῃ Δεῖ τὸν υἱὸν τοῦ ἀνθρώπου ἀποδοκιμασθῆναι, ὑβρισθῆναι, σταυρωθῆναι, ὡς περὶ ἄλλου φαίνεται λέγων, δηλονότι τοῦ ἐμπαθοῦς· Καὶ προάξω ὑμᾶς, λέγει, τῇ τρίτῃ τῶν ἡμερῶν εἰς τὴν Γαλιλαίαν· αὐτὸς γὰρ προάγει πάντα καὶ τὴν ἀφανῶς σωζομένην ψυχὴν ἀναστήσειν ἠνίσσετο καὶ ἀποκαταστήσειν οὗ νῦν προάγει ἀπέθανεν δὲ ἀποστάντος τοῦ καταβάντος ἐπ᾽ αὐτῷ ἐπὶ τῷ Ἰορδάνῃ πνεύματος ἀναστείλας τὴν ἐπελθοῦσαν ἀκτῖνα τῆς δυνάμεως ὁ Σωτὴρ ἀπείλησε μὲν τὸν θάνατον τὸ δὲ θνητὸν σῶμα ἀποβαλὼν πάθη ἀνέστησεν. τὰ ψυχικὰ μὲν οὖν οὕτως ἀνίσταται καὶ ἀνασώζεται ..κάθηται μὲν οὖν ὁ ψυχικὸς Χριστὸς ἐν δεξιᾷ τοῦ δημιουργοῦ (§§ 61, 62).

The last of these extracts appears to represent Western rathei than Eastern Valentinianism, a member of the Anatolic school would have spoken of the Risen Christ as 'pneumatic' and not 'psychic' But the point is not important for our present purpose We see how a Valentinian writer could make the facts of the Gospel history the vehicle of Gnostic teaching, and we understand why the Docetic author of the Petrine Gospel was content to accept the canonical narrative as the basis of his own. But besides this, we recognise in these Valentinian comments points of contact with our fragment where the latter reveals its true character We observe in both the same distinction between the Impassible Christ and the Passible, in both the Power from above leaves the Lord at His death, in both there is a Resurrection effectuated by an external agency and apparently not extending to the natural Body. Both again are characterised by the prominence which is given to the Cross and to the Preaching to the Dead, although neither of these particulars is worked out in the same way by the two writers. On the whole, while the evidence does not justify us in regarding the Petrine writer as a Valentinian, there is reason to suppose that he has felt the influence of the Valentinian School.

4. Both Clement of Alexandria and Hippolytus speak of a party who bore the name of Docetae, and who are distinguished from the

Valentinians and other Gnostic sects   According to Clement[1], the founder of this party was Julius Cassianus, originally a member of one of the Valentinian schools.   Cassian shared Tatian's Encratism, and his interest in Docetism appears to have been largely due to his Encratite views.   Hippolytus[2] attributes to the later Docetae, presumably the sect which Cassian originated or one nearly allied to it, an elaborate system of gnosis, which combines features apparently derived from several earlier systems, as those of Basilides, Valentinus, and the Naassenes   When we come to the Christology of these Docetae, it proves to be a curious syncretism presenting points of contact with orthodoxy on the one hand, and with many forms of Gnostic speculation on the other.   The higher Nature of Christ is the Only Begotten Son, Who is equal in all respects (generation excepted) to the Ingenerate   The Only Begotten contracts Himself and descends through the Aeons, till at length He enters the world and is born of Mary.   The Docetic writer proceeds ·

ἐγεννήθη τὸ ἐξ αὐτῆς ὡς γέγραπται   γεννηθὲν δὲ ἐνεδύσατο αὐτὸ ἄνωθεν ἐλθών, καὶ πάντα ἐποίησεν οὕτως ὡς ἐν τοῖς εὐαγγελίοις γέγραπται. ἐλούσατο εἰς τὸν Ἰορδάνην   ἐλούσατο δὲ τύπον καὶ σφράγισμα λαβὼν ἐν τῷ ὕδατι τοῦ γεγεννημένου σώματος ἀπὸ τῆς παρθένου, ἵν' ὅταν ὁ ἄρχων κατακρίνῃ τὸ ἴδιον πλάσμα θανάτῳ τῷ σταυρῷ, ψυχὴ ἐκείνη ἐν τῷ σώματι τραφεῖσα ἀπεκδυσαμένη τὸ σῶμα.. μὴ εὑρεθῇ γυμνή, ἀλλ' ἐνδύσηται τὸ ἐν τῷ ὕδατι ὅτε ἐβαπτίζετο ἀντὶ τῆς σαρκὸς ἐκείνης ἐκτετυπωμένον σῶμα.

Unfortunately the Hippolytean account breaks off at this point   Its importance for our enquiry lies in the witness which it bears to the existence of a party in the second half of the second century (for the syncretistic spirit it displayed cannot have been earlier) who called themselves Docetae but accepted the Gospel narrative, and whose δόκησις was apparently limited to a belief in a pneumatic Body, the impress or counterpart of the Body born of the Virgin, which was acquired by the Lord at the Baptism, and remained as the clothing of His soul after the Crucifixion.   There is no evidence that this particular theory was

[1] Clem. Alex. iii. 13 τοιούτοις ἐπιχειρεῖ καὶ ὁ τῆς δοκήσεως ἐξάρχων Ἰούλιος Κασσιανός.
[2] Hipp. viii. 10 sqq. Hippolytus plays all round the name, but seems not to perceive its true significance: viii 8 ἐπεὶ οἱ πολλοὶ τῇ τοῦ κυρίου συνβουλίᾳ μὴ χρώμενοι τὴν δοκὸν ἐν τῷ ὀφθαλμῷ ἔχοντες ὁρᾶν ἐπαγγέλλονται τυφλώττοντες, δοκεῖ

ἡμῖν μηδὲ τὰ τούτων δόγματα σιωπᾶν καὶ τοὺς τῷ δοκεῖν ἀσφάλειαν λόγων κεκτῆσθαι ἐλέγξομεν, οἵγε ἑαυτοὺς Δοκητὰς ἀπεκάλεσαν, δογματίζοντες ταῦτα (cf. ib. 11 τὸ δοκεῖν εἶναί τινας   τὰ δόξαντα). His statement that the name proceeded from the party itself is of a piece with the explanation of its meaning

present to the mind of the Petrine writer, but it is not inconsistent with his story, nor does there appear to be any improbability in the supposition that the Encratite sect founded in Egypt by Julius Cassianus, the Docetae of Hippolytus, and the Docetae of Serapion were closely allied to each other if not identically the same.

IX.

The style of the Petrine fragment has points of contact with the canonical Gospels, especially with St Luke and St John, yet on the whole it differs materially   Here and there the writer uses a phrase of Aramaic origin such as μία τῶν ἀζύμων, ἀνὰ δύο δύο. More frequently he manifests a tendency to substitute classical for Hellenistic forms.   Thus he writes καθαρεύω for ἀθῶός εἰμι ἀπό, and employs the optative after ὅπως   In his choice of words he appears to be guided by such writers as Plutarch, Polybius, Dionysius of Halicarnassus; we have ὄψεις for ὀφθαλμοί, ἀγωνιᾶν for φοβεῖσθαι followed by μή, and the phrases φλέγεσθαι ὑπὸ ὀργῆς, τετρῶσθαι κατὰ διάνοιαν. In common with the author of the Acts, whose work seems to be often in view, Peter uses μαθήτρια and χειραγωγεῖν, with Symmachus, the perhaps heretical translator of the Old Testament, he shares the very rare words ὑπορθοῦν and συνσκέπτεσθαι   He shews a partiality for unusual words: for σταυρίσκειν and σκελοκοπεῖν he is as yet our only authority, ὑπακοή in the sense of a 'response' does not seem to occur elsewhere before the last years of the third century, although ὑπακούειν 'to respond' is found in other apocryphal writings of the second, λαχμός is in itself a rare word, and in the phrase λαχμὸν βάλλειν seems to be limited to two or three Christian writers   A characteristic habit of affixing an almost otiose ἐκεῖνος (οἱ κακοῦργοι ἐκεῖνοι, ὁ λίθος ἐκεῖνος, οἱ στρατιῶται ἐκεῖνοι) appears also in the Petrine Apocalypse, and in other apocryphal literature.   But the most decisive indication of the relatively late composition of our fragment is to be found in its use of ἡ κυριακή.   In the Apocalypse of St John we already have ἡ κυριακὴ ἡμέρα, the *Didache* follows with κυριακὴ Κυρίου, Ignatius speaks of those who live κατὰ κυριακήν, Melito, Bishop of Sardis, about the middle of the second century wrote a treatise περὶ κυριακῆς.   The name was therefore familiar amongst Eastern Greek-speaking Christians from the end of the first century.   But Peter not only uses it freely, but seems to be unconscious that he is guilty of an anachronism when he imports this exclusively Christian term into the Gospel history.   Ἡ κυριακή has so completely supplanted ἡ μία τῶν σαββάτων, that it is twice used to describe the first Easter Day in a document which usually manifests precision in such matters

A more vital distinction between the literary character of the Petrine fragment and that of the canonical Gospels lies in the assumption of the first person by the writer of the former. The design of the Synoptic Gospels excludes personal narrative, but it is equally foreign to the Fourth Gospel, even where reference is made to the evangelist as an eye-witness (xix 35, xx 30, 31) The method of putting the Gospel-history into the mouth of an Apostle belongs to a type of literature later than the canonical Gospels Zahn remarks that the first specimen of the kind hitherto known is to be found in the *Gospel of the Twelve*, an Ebionite *apocryphon* which was circulated in Palestine probably about A D 170[1] The *Didascalia* and the *Constitutions* furnish later examples.

X

We may now approach the question of locality and date. Where and when was the Gospel of Peter written?

1. All the evidence points to Western Syria as the place of origin. The Gospel was read at Rhosus in the time of Serapion In the next century it was in the hands of the author of the *Didascalia*, and of Origen during his residence in Palestine. Its name and general character were familiar to Eusebius of Caesarea, Cyril of Jerusalem had studied its contents, Theodoret of Cyrrhus knew of its existence No Western writer shews any independent knowledge of the Petrine Gospel, unless it be Jerome, who like Origen lived for years in Palestine. The discovery of a fragment of the Gospel in the grave of an Egyptian monk proves nothing as to a circulation of the Gospel in Egypt. The writer was in possession of a few leaves only, and the leaves or the copy from which they were detached may have been brought to the Thebaid by some exile from Syria. It will be remembered with interest that in his last wanderings Nestorius paid more than one visit to Panopolis[2].

2. The Gospel of Peter was in use about the year 190, and, according to Serapion, it was the work of at least a generation earlier. Thus the *terminus ad quem* may be fixed at A D 170. The other limit is more difficult to determine. Yet if the evidence already produced is

---

[1] *Das Ev. des Petrus*, p 17, cf *Gesch. des N T. Kanons*, ii. 2, p 725.   [2] Evagr Schol i 7

trustworthy, it can scarcely be rash to say that the Gospel, so far as it may be judged by the fragment which survives, was not written before the middle of the second century. The Akhmîm fragment presupposes a knowledge and use of the Four Gospels, and of a text of the Gospels which is already marked by a characteristic interpolation[1]. Its author seems to have had access to a Harmony nearly akin to Tatian's Diatessaron If he is not actually indebted to Justin, he is versed in the apologetic use of certain passages of the Old Testament which was prevalent among literary Christians from Justin's time Above all, his doctrinal affinities are those of the second half of the second century His Docetism is not of the type which was familiar to Ignatius, his Gnosticism connects itself with the schools of Valentinus and Julius Cassianus, his anti-Judaic spirit is worthy of Marcion, his apocalyptic tone finds its nearest parallels in the literature which passes under the name of Leucius Charinus The conditions are those of the age which followed Justin, and not of that which preceded him. We shall not perhaps be wide of the mark if we place the composition of the Petrine Gospel midway between the limits already indicated, i.e. about A D 165, we cannot, consistently with our reading of the facts, place it before A D 150.

XI.

On his journey up the Nile, between Assiout and Abu Girgeh, the traveller passes on the East bank, at a little distance from the stream, the large market town of Akhmîm. It marks the site of one of the oldest cities of the Thebaid, the Chemmis of Herodotus (II. 91), the Panopolis of Strabo (XVII. p 812) Once the stronghold of the worship of Khem, identified with the Greek Pan, Panopolis became in Christian times a centre of monastic life. An extensive Christian necropolis, begun in the fifth century, bears witness to the ecclesiastical importance of the place in days before the Arab invasion, and Akhmîm is said to contain at the present time a relatively large proportion of Christian inhabitants.

During the winter of 1886—7 the researches of the French Archaeological Mission in Egypt led to the discovery in one of the graves of Christian Panopolis of a small book measuring 6 inches by $4\frac{1}{2}$, and containing 33 leaves of parchment, stitched together into covers of pasteboard roughly cased in leather. The book was found to contain

---

[1] That the interpolation in Luke xxiii. 48 originated with Peter is improbable Peter puts it into the mouth of the elders, changing the connexion after his usual manner of dealing with evangelical materials

fragments of the lost Petrine Gospel and Apocalypse, and of the Greek version of the Book of Enoch , on the inside of the further cover was pasted a single leaf of the Greek Acts of St Julian   The Petrine writings occupy the first nine leaves.   The *recto* of the first leaf bears a Coptic cross supported by A and Ω , the fragment of the Gospel begins under a smaller cross on the second page, ending on fol 5*b*, where its conclusion is marked by three crosses resting on an ornamental band.   A blank leaf follows the Gospel, which is succeeded by the fragment of the Apocalypse   The latter has either been stitched into the volume upside down, or the gathering has been turned by the writer , the two fragments are in the same hand and were probably written about the same time   The writing will be described presently ; meanwhile it may be remarked that it can be distinguished at a glance from the hands in which Enoch and the fragment of the Acts have been written   The rest of the book is in uncial characters which appear to be those of the seventh or eighth century , the Petrine fragments are written in a cursive script of a peculiar type, probably belonging to the same period   It is worthy of notice that while each of the Petrine fragments is followed by a blank, as if the writer had stopped because he had reached the end of his copy, there is no such blank between the fragments of the Enoch or at the end of the Codex.   It would seem as if the writer of the Petrine matter having in his possession some leaves of Enoch which were nearly of the same size with his 'Peter,' bound the whole together   At the death of the writer (or of the last owner of the book, if it fell into other hands) the precious collection was buried with him.   From the position of the grave, M. Bouriant infers that the burial took place not before the beginning of the eighth century, nor after the end of the twelfth

The palaeographical features which distinguish the Petrine fragments are well defined   The writing is that of a rapid writer who seems unwilling to lift his hand from the parchment.   We notice at times the characteristic 'linking' of the letters which marks the papyrus cursive   Many of the letters preserve the uncial form, e g. Γ, Δ, H, M, N, P, C, Y. But the writer's practice is not uniform, thus Δ occasionally appears almost in the form of d, and H becomes h.   ι is often inordinately long, κ takes the shape of k, c is large and singularly formed.   The writing is either nearly perpendicular or inclines slightly to the left.   Some of the peculiarities in detail occur also in the Akhmîm mathematical papyrus, which M. Baillet ascribes to century vii—viii.   But in its general effect, so far as a judgement can be based upon a comparison of the lithographed specimens of the papyrus with the heliotype of the Petrine fragments, the writing of the latter is quite distinct, the hand is freer, bolder, and more suggestive of the rapid execution of a practised scribe. M. Lods points out that the writer of the Petrine fragments has used the familiar abbreviations $\overline{a\nu o s}$, $\overline{\kappa s}$, $\overline{\theta s}$, and the horizontal bar for the final ν In one instance a dative is followed by the ι ascript, once also an apostrophe occurs at the end of a proper name, double dots are occasionally placed over ι and ν, and once over η There are no breathings or accents, and no stops, except a colon which is said to mark the end of the fragment, but does not appear in the heliograph.

The MS in places has suffered from damp The first lines of ff 1 *b*, 2*a*, and the words lying nearest to the right hand margin of ff 2*a*, 3*b*, 4*a*, are from this cause more or less difficult to decipher For words or portions of words which are illegible in the heliotype, I have been compelled, with M Lods, to trust to M Bouriant's reading of the MS ; these are indicated by being inclosed in square brackets in the lower margin of the text. An insect has gnawed through the first leaf, destroying the tops of some of the letters in f. 1 *b*, line 2, happily the restoration here proposed by M Lods is scarcely open to doubt. At the beginning of f 5*b* the writing suddenly becomes lighter and finer, and continues so throughout the page, but the difference appears to be due merely to a change of pen.

There is some reason to think that the parchment had been at least in places previously occupied by other writing. Traces of an earlier cursive hand are here and there discoverable.

XII.

A considerable literature has already begun to spring up round the Petrine fragments. The following are the most important editions of the fragment of the Gospel and books connected with it

Mémoires publiés par les membres de la Mission Archéologique Française au Caire sous la direction de M U Bouriant Tome neuvième, 1er fascicule, 1892 : 3e fascicule, 1893 Paris Ernest Leroux

The Apocryphal Gospel of Peter: the Greek text of the newly discovered fragment London : Macmillan and Co, 1892. Revised edition with some corrections from the MS, 1893.

The Gospel according to Peter and the Revelation of Peter. Two lectures by J. Armitage Robinson, B D, and M R James, M A. London C. J. Clay and Sons, 1892. Second edition, 1892

A popular account of the newly recovered Gospel of St Peter   By J Rendel Harris. London: Hodder and Stoughton, 1892.

Evangelii secundum Petrum et Petri Apocalypseos quae supersunt . .edidit Adolphe Lods. Parisiis ap. Ern Leroux, 1892.

Bruchstucke des Evangeliums und der Apokalypse des Petrus, von Adolf Harnack   Leipzig· J. C Hinrichs, 1893   Second edition, 1893.

Das Evangelium des Petrus, von D. Theodor Zahn. Erlangen u. Leipzig· A Deichert, 1893 [1].

Important contributions to the subject will be found in the *Guardian* (Dec. 7, 14, 1892), *Academy* (Dec 10, 17, 24, 1892), *Athenæum* (Dec. 17, 1892, May 13, 1893), *Expositor* (Jan., 1893), *Classical Review* (Feb , 1893), *Scottish Guardian* (Feb. 24, &c , 1893), *Preussische Jahrbucher* (Jan , 1893), *Theol Literaturzeitung* (Dec. 10, 1892, Jan. 21, Apr 1, 1893), *Theol. Tijdschrift* (May, 1893).

---

[1] In the critical notes the following abbreviations have been used   B = Bouriant, H = Harnack, L = Lods, R = Robinson, Z = Zahn.

ΕΥΑΓΓΕΛΙΟΝ ΚΑΤΑ ΠΕΤΡΟΝ

I. Τῶν δὲ Ἰουδαίων οὐδεὶς ἐνίψατο τὰς χεῖρας, οὐδὲ Ἡρῴδης οὐδ᾽ εἷς τῶν κριτῶν αὐτοῦ· καὶ μὴ βουληθέντων νίψασθαι ἀνέστη Πειλᾶτος. καὶ τότε

1 τ[ων]   2 εἶς is uncertain : ουδ εις has perhaps been corrected to ουδε τις   2—3 Parts of the letters represented by καὶ μὴ β have been destroyed remaining traces support the reading adopted   3 Πειλατης

1. τῶν δὲ Ἰουδαίων κ.τ λ.] The callousness of the Jewish leaders is sharply contrasted with the scruples of the Gentile Procurator. *Didasc.* v. 19 ὁ μὲν ἀλλόφυλος κριτὴς νιψάμενος τὰς χεῖρας εἶπεν Ἀθῷός εἰμι ὁ δὲ Ἰσραὴλ ἐπεβόησε Τὸ αἷμα αὐτοῦ ἐφ᾽ ἡμᾶς. Οἱ Ἰουδαῖοι are more especially the Pharisees and priestly party (comp. Pet vii); the phrase is from St John (i. 19, &c) Ἐνίψατο Matt xxvii 24 ἀπενίψατο· The simple verb is used also in *Didasc. l. c.* and *Ev. Nicod* 1 (B) 10 νιπτόμενος τὰς χεῖρας.

2 οὐδ᾽ εἷς τῶν κριτῶν αὐτοῦ κ.τ λ.] 'Nor yet any one of His judges,' 1 e, the members of the Sanhedrin who had condemned Him (Mark xiv. 64) On οὐδὲ εἷς see Winer-Moulton, 216, *n.* 2 for οὐδεὶς οὐδὲ...οὐδέ Zahn compares Mark xiii 32. Καὶ μὴ βουληθέντων see the critical note. The reluctance was significant ; cf. Mark vii. 3 οἱ γὰρ Φαρισαῖοι.. ἐὰν μὴ πυγμῇ νίψωνται τὰς χεῖρας οὐκ ἐσθίουσιν. Origen. *Matt* 124 "et ipse quidem se lauit, illi autem non solum se mundare noluerunt a sanguine

Christi, sed etiam super se susceperunt."

3 Since no one chose to follow his example, Pilate rose up from the βῆμα; his part in the trial was over. Cf. Acts xxvi. 30 ἀνέστη τε ὁ βασιλεὺς καὶ ὁ ἡγεμών. "And then" (καὶ τότε occurs again c. vi.) Herod assumes the *rôle* of judge, and orders that the prisoner be taken over (παραλημφθῆναι, comp Matt xxvii 27 οἱ στρατιῶται . . παραλαβόντες τὸν Ἰησοῦν ; *infra,* c. iii) The object is to minimise the sin of the Procurator by laying the chief guilt at the door of Herod, the representative of the Jews (1, 2) Peter remembers that the Lord was ἐκ τῆς ἐξουσίας Ἡρῴδου (Luke xxiii. 7). He remembers also Ps. ii. 2 οἱ βασιλεῖς τῆς γῆς καὶ οἱ ἄρχοντες συνήχθησαν κ.τ.λ., together with the comment in Acts. iv. 27 συνήχθησαν γὰρ ἐπ᾽ ἀληθείας Ἡρῴδης τε καὶ Πόντιος Πειλᾶτος. The *Didascalia* follows Peter (v. 19 Ἡ. ὁ βασιλεὺς ἐκέλευσεν αὐτὸν σταυρωθῆναι); in the *Constitutions* the sentence is recast to save the appearance of a conflict with the canonical Gospels II. ὁ ἡγεμὼν

S P

I

κελεύει Ἡρῴδης ὁ βασιλεὺς παραλημφθῆναι τὸν κύριον,
εἰπὼν αὐτοῖς ὅτι "Οσα ἐκέλευσα ὑμῖν ποιῆσαι αὐτῷ,
ποιήσατε.

II.   Ἱστήκει δὲ ἐκεῖ Ἰωσὴφ ὁ φίλος Πειλάτου
καὶ τοῦ κυρίου, καὶ εἰδὼς ὅτι σταυρίσκειν αὐτὸν μέλ- 5
λουσιν, ἦλθεν πρὸς τὸν Πειλᾶτον καὶ ᾔτησε τὸ σῶμα
τοῦ κυρίου πρὸς ταφήν. καὶ ὁ Πειλᾶτος πέμψας πρὸς
Ἡρῴδην ᾔτησεν αὐτοῦ τὸ σῶμα, καὶ ὁ Ἡρῴδης ἔφη
Ἀδελφὲ Πειλᾶτε, εἰ καὶ μή τις αὐτὸν ᾐτήκει, ἡμεῖς

1 παρ[αλη]μφθῆναι

καὶ Ἡ. ὁ βασιλεὺς ἐκέλευσαν   ᾽Ο
βασιλεὺς Ἡ. = ὁ τετραάρχης occurs in
Mark vi. 14 (cf Matt xiv. 9).

2. "Οσα ἐκέλευσα ὑμῖν κ.τλ.] This
order is possibly intended to include
the mockery. Herod's words may
refer to an earlier portion of the
Petrine narrative based upon Luke
xxiii 11 (ἐξουθενήσας)

4 ἱστήκει δὲ ἐκεῖ Ἰωσὴφ κ.τ.λ]
Meanwhile Joseph, who had antici-
pated the sentence, was standing
near the spot (cf. John xviii 16 ὁ δὲ
Πέτρος ἱστήκει πρὸς τῇ θύρᾳ ἔξω xix
25 ἱστήκεισαν δὲ παρὰ τῷ σταυρῷ κ τ λ),
ready to prefer his request.   Ἀπὸ
Ἀριμαθαίας (Mt., Mk , L , J) is wanting
in Peter, and its place is filled by ὁ
φίλος Π. καὶ τοῦ κυρίου. For Joseph's
connexion with Christ see Matt.
xxvii. 57 ἐμαθητεύθη τῷ Ἰησοῦ, John
xix 38 ὢν μαθητὴς τοῦ Ἰησοῦ κεκρυμ-
μένος, and Pet. vi. His acquaintance with Pilate may have been
inferred from his wealth and position (πλούσιος, Mt., εὐσχήμων βουλευτής, Mk.), or from his boldness,
a different account is given of the
τόλμα in Ev Nicod i. (Β) 11 Pilate
is again placed in a favourable light;
he is a friend of the Lord's friend,
and he endorses Joseph's request,

sending it on to Herod as the
person who possesses jurisdiction.
Ἥτησε Mt , Mk , L , ᾐτήσατο , J ,
ἠρώτησεν. Σταυρίσκειν is unknown to
the lexicons ; σταυρώσειν has been
proposed, but perhaps unnecessarily.
7 Πρὸς ταφήν comp Matt. xxvii.
7 εἰς ταφήν
9 Ἀδελφὲ Πειλᾶτε κ.τ.λ.] Luke
xxiii. 12 ἐγένοντο φίλοι.   In his
reply Herod identifies himself with
the Jews 'although no one had
asked for Him, we (ἡμεῖς) should
bury Him (for the construction cf.
John xix 11 οὐκ εἶχες ἐξουσίαν...εἰ μὴ
ἦν δεδόμενον) ; our law forbids us to
let the sun go down on the unburied
corpse of a murdered man ; and on
this occasion we should be the more
careful, since (ἐπεὶ καὶ) the Sabbath
is coming on.'   For ἐπιφώσκειν in
this sense comp Luke xxiii. 54 ἡμέρα
ἦν παρασκευῆς καὶ σάββατον ἐπέφωσκεν ;
and Pet ix. τῇ νυκτὶ ᾗ ἐπέφωσκεν ἡ
κυριακή.   Peter seems to refer to
John xix. 31 οἱ μὲν οὖν Ἰουδαῖοι, ἐπεὶ
παρασκευὴ ἦν, ἵνα μὴ μείνῃ ἐπὶ τοῦ
σταυροῦ τὰ σώματα ἐν τῷ σαββάτῳ ..
ἠρώτησαν τὸν Πειλᾶτον ἵνα κατεαγῶσιν
αὐτῶν τὰ σκέλη καὶ ἀρθῶσιν It is remarkable that the Peshitto works
into this verse the Petrine phrase

αὐτὸν ἐθάπτομεν, ἐπεὶ καὶ σάββατον ἐπιφώσκει·
γέγραπται γὰρ ἐν τῷ νόμῳ ἥλιον μὴ δῦναι ἐπὶ πεφονευμένῳ. III. Καὶ παρέδωκεν αὐτὸν τῷ λαῷ πρὸ μιᾶς τῶν
5 ἀζύμων, τῆς ἑορτῆς αὐτῶν. οἱ δὲ λαβόντες τὸν κύριον

5 τον κυ

ἐπεὶ σάββατον ἐπιφώσκει, rendering
ἐν τῷ σαββάτῳ by ܟ݁ܕ݂ܶܪ̈ܬܐ ܐܠܦܐ,
ܟ݁ܢܫܐ without support from any
Greek MS So too the Arabic Diatessaron 2. γέγραπται γὰρ ἐν τῷ νόμῳ] Deut.
XXI. 23, LXX. οὐ κοιμηθήσεται τὸ σῶμα
αὐτοῦ ἐπὶ τοῦ ξύλου, ἀλλὰ ταφῇ θάψετε
αὐτὸ ἐν τῇ ἡμέρᾳ ἐκείνῃ. Similarly
Aq, Symm., Theod. Peter has read
into this text the interpretation given
to it by the precedent of Jos x 27
πρὸς ἡλίου δυσμὰς καθεῖλον αὐτοὺς
ἀπὸ τῶν ξύλων. The Constitutions follow Peter (v 14 θάπτεται πρὸ ἡλίου
δύσεως), and Epiphanius (haer 66,
79) even cites the Deuteronomic
law in this form ἔλεγεν ὁ νόμος .. οὐ
μὴ δύνῃ ὁ ἥλιος ἐπ' αὐτῷ .. θάψαντες
θάψατε αὐτὸν πρὸ δύσεως τοῦ ἡλίου.
The gloss can however be traced
back to Philo and Josephus ; cf Phil
de spec. legg. 28 φησί Μὴ ἐπιδυέτω ὁ
ἥλιος ἀνεσκολοπισμένοις, ἀλλ' ἐπικρυπ-
τέσθωσαν γῇ πρὸ δύσεως καθαιρεθέντες.
Jos. B. J. iv 5 12 προσῆλθον δὲ εἰς
τοσοῦτον ἀσεβείας ὥστε καὶ ἀτάφους
ῥίψαι, καίτοι τοσαύτην Ἰουδαίων περὶ
τὰς ταφὰς πρόνοιαν ποιουμένων ὥστε
καὶ τοὺς ἐκ καταδίκης ἀνασταυρουμένους
πρὸ δύντος ἡλίου καθελεῖν τε καὶ
θάψαι. Πεφονευμένῳ is strangely
attributed to Herod, from whom we
should have expected κεκρεμασμένῳ or
the like , but it agrees with the anti-
Judaic tone of the fragment. The Crucifixion was a judicial murder ; Acts
vii 52 τοῦ δικαίου .. φονεῖς ἐγένεσθε.
James v. 6 ἐφονεύσατε τὸν δίκαιον.
4. καὶ παρέδωκεν αὐτὸν κ.τ.λ.] "And

he delivered Him to the people before the first day of unleavened bread,
their feast " Παρέδωκεν is in Mt , L.,
J , but the person who delivers the
Lord is in the canonical Gospels Pilate ; in Peter, Herod. The surrender
is to the people, who share the guilt
of their leaders (Matt xxvii. 25 πᾶς ὁ
λαός). Πρὸ μιᾶς τῶν ἀζύμων = πρὸ πρώ-
της τ. ἀζ. (Matt xxvi. 17, Mark xiv.
12). Peter follows St John's reckoning and makes the first day of the
Passover correspond with the Sabbath, and the Crucifixion precede it.
Τῆς ἑορτῆς αὐτῶν also is Johannine,
cf. John vi 4 τὸ πάσχα ἡ ἑορτὴ τῶν
Ἰουδαίων ; also v. 1, vii. 2 From Peter
the phrase has found its way into
the Didascalia v 15 ἐν αὐτῇ γὰρ ἐν
μέσῳ αὐτῶν τῆς ἑορτῆς τῶν ἀζύμων
ἐσταύρωσάν με, κατὰ τὸ προειρημένον
ὑπὸ Δαβὶδ Ἔθεντο τὰ σημεῖα αὐτῶν ἐν
μέσῳ τῆς ἑορτῆς αὐτῶν (Ps lxxiii. =
lxxiv 4, 5). Since the MSS of the
LXX seem invariably to read ἐν μέσῳ
τῆς ἑορτῆς σου, it appears that the
Didascalia, followed by the Constitutions (v 15), has imported the Petrine phrase into the Psalm ; unless
the change belongs to a primitive
interpretation of the Psalm anterior
both to the Didascalia and to Peter.
    In Peter τῆς ἑορτῆς αὐτῶν makes
a fresh point against the Jews ; they
committed the murder on the eve of
their greatest sacred festival.
    5. οἱ δὲ λαβόντες τὸν κύριον κ.τ.λ.]
The λαός are the subject, for λαβόντες
takes up παρέδωκεν—comp. John xix.
16, 17 παρέδωκεν αὐτὸν αὐτοῖς (=τοῖς
Ἰουδαίοις, cf. 14)...παρέλαβον οὖν τὸν

1—2

ὤθουν αὐτὸν τρέχοντες, καὶ ἔλεγον Σύρωμεν τὸν υἱὸν
τοῦ θεοῦ, ἐξουσίαν αὐτοῦ ἐσχηκότες. καὶ πορφύραν
αὐτὸν περιέβαλλον, καὶ ἐκάθισαν αὐτὸν ἐπὶ καθέδραν
κρίσεως, λέγοντες Δικαίως κρῖνε, βασιλεῦ τοῦ Ἰσραήλ.
καί τις αὐτῶν ἐνεγκὼν στέφανον ἀκάνθινον ἔθηκεν ἐπὶ 5

1 αυτων

Ἰησοῦν. The soldiers are not mentioned by Peter even at the Crucifixion, the Jews being regarded as
the real executioners, comp St
Peter's words in Acts ii 23 διὰ
χειρὸς ἀνόμων προσπήξαντες ἀνείλατε.
Ὤθουν αὐτὸν τρέχοντες suggests that
what follows takes place on the way
to the Cross, which otherwise finds
no place in Peter ; yet some of the
details, e.g the placing of the Lord on
the καθέδρα, look the other way. The
whole scene is in fact foreshortened
without regard to historical accuracy. The eagerness of the per-
secutors implied by τρέχοντες was
perhaps no uncommon featuie in
the experience of the second century comp. mart. Polyc. 7 ἐξῆλθον
ὡς ἐπὶ λῃστὴν τρέχοντες—the spectators wondering why theie was
τοσαύτη σπουδὴ. τοῦ συλληφθῆναι
τοιοῦτον πρεσβύτην ἄνδρα.
1. Σύρωμεν κτλ] The sequence
ὤθουν.. καὶ ἔλεγον Σ is not very felici-
tous. But σύρειν was familiarized by
its use in the Acts (viii 3, xiv. 9, xvii.
6), and is employed on similar occa-
sions by other apocryphal writers,
e g Acta Philippi 15 βιαίως καὶ ἀπαν-
θρώπως συρομένων αὐτῶν. Comp
Epiph haer. 76. 1 συρέντος ὅλην σχεδὸν
τὴν πόλιν καὶ οὕτως ἀποθανόντος With
ἐξ. αὐτοῦ ἐσχηκότες comp. John xix. 10,
11.
2. πορφύραν αὐτὸν περιέβαλλον]
Mark xv 17 ἐνδιδύσκουσιν αὐτὸν πορφύραν. Luke xxiii. 11 περιβαλὼν
ἐσθῆτα λαμπράν John xix 2 ἱμάτιον
πορφυροῦν περιέβαλον αὐτόν.
3. ἐκάθισαν αὐτὸν ἐπὶ καθέδραν

κρίσεως κ.τ.λ.] Possibly based upon
John xix. 13 ὁ οὖν Πειλᾶτος ἤγαγεν
ἔξω τὸν Ἰησοῦν, καὶ ἐκάθισεν ἐπὶ βήματος for καθίζειν trans. comp. 1 Cor.
vi 4, Eph i 20. The reference to
St John seems to be more direct in
Justin apol 1 35 καὶ γὰρ (ὡς εἶπεν ὁ
προφήτης) διασύροντες αὐτὸν ἐκάθισαν
ἐπὶ βήματος, καὶ εἶπον Κρῖνον ἡμῖν
Yet Justin refers to 'the Prophet,'
i e. Isaiah lviii. 2 (a passage which
he has just quoted) αἰτοῦσίν με νῦν
κρίσιν δικαίαν Peter avoids βῆμα, pre-
ferring perhaps a word of Jewish as-
sociations (Ps.cvi (cvii)32 ἐν καθέδραις
πρεσβυτέρων, Matt xxiii. 2 ἐπὶ τῆς
Μωυσέως καθέδρας), and if he has a
prophecy in view, it may be Ps lxxi.
(lxxii.) 1, 2 ὁ θεός, τὸ κρίμα σου τῷ
βασιλεῖ δὸς κρίνειν τὸν λαόν σου ἐν
δικαιοσύνη. In Prov. xxiv. 77 (xxxi. 9)
we have the exact phrase κρῖνε δικαίως, Harnack (Bruchstucke, p. 25)
points out that this combination
appears also in 1 Pet ii. 23, and compares John vii. 24. Βασιλεῦ τῶν
Ἰουδαίων is the title used by the
mockers in Mt , Mk , J ; Peter writes
τοῦ Ἰσραήλ both here and below,
c iv , comp. Matt. xxvii 42, John
xii. 13.

5 καί τις αὐτῶν ἐνεγκὼν κ.τ.λ.]
Petei individualizes where the Synoptic Gospels speak generally ; so
below (c. v.) καί τις αὐτῶν εἶπεν
Ποτίσατε αὐτόν. For στέφανον ἀκάνθινον ἔθηκεν comp Mark xv. 17 πε-
ριτιθέασιν αὐτῷ πλέξαντες ἀκάνθινον
στέφανον. Ἐνέπτυον is from Mark
xv. 19, ἐράπισαν from Matt xxvi. 68
(John xix. 3). Ταῖς ὄψεσιν corre-

τῆς κεφαλῆς τοῦ κυρίου· καὶ ἕτεροι ἑστῶτες ἐνέπτυον
αὐτοῦ ταῖς ὄψεσι, καὶ ἄλλοι τὰς σιαγόνας αὐτοῦ
ἐράπισαν· ἕτεροι καλάμῳ ἔνυσσον αὐτόν, καί τινες
αὐτὸν ἐμάστιζον λέγοντες Ταύτῃ τῇ τιμῇ τιμήσωμεν
5 τὸν υἱὸν τοῦ θεοῦ.   IV. Καὶ ἤνεγκον δύο κακούργους, καὶ ἐσταύρωσαν
ἀνὰ μέσον αὐτῶν τὸν κύριον· αὐτὸς δὲ ἐσιώπα, ὡς μηδὲν

1 καὶ ἕτεροι...ὄψεσι καὶ] For the most part illegible in the heliotype
2 σιαγόνας ἐράπισαν. obscure   6 ην[εγκον]   7 αυτ[ων τον κυ] | μηδένα R, L.

sponds to εἰς τὸ πρόσωπον αὐτοῦ,
Matt. xxvi. 67, for αἱ ὄψεις=οἱ
ὀφθαλμοί, comp. Zahn, *Acta Joannis*,
248 ὁ ἐπανοίξας μου τοῦ νοῦ τὰς ὄψεις
Polyb. 3 79. 12 ἐστερήθη τῆς μιᾶς
ὄψεως. Plutarch. *symp*. i. p 615 D
κύκλῳ ταῖς ὄψεσιν ἐπελθὼν τοὺς κατα-
κειμένους. Euseb. *in Esa*. liii 5 τὰς
ὄψεις ῥαπιζόμενος. Τὰς σιαγόνας may
look back to Matt v 39 ὅστις σε
ῥαπίζει εἰς τὴν δεξιὰν σιαγόνα κ.τ.λ.,
but more probably rests directly on
Isaiah l. 6 τὰς δὲ σιαγόνας μου εἰς
ῥαπίσματα [ἔδωκα]. Καλάμῳ ἔνυσσον
gives a new turn to the canonical
ἔτυπτον.. καλάμῳ (Mark xv. 19, cf
Matt. xxvii. 30), combining it with
λόγχῃ ἔνυξεν (John xix 34); cf *Orac.
Sibyll* viii. 296 πλευρὰς νύξουσιν καλάμῳ Lastly, ἐμάστιζον seems to refer
to John xix 1 ὁ Πειλᾶτος.. ἐμαστίγωσεν—so serious a punishment was
kept by the Procurator in his own
hands, but Peter attributes it to the
Jews, in agreement with Mark x 34,
&c For the form μαστίζειν see Acts
xxii. 25, and comp *Constitutions*, v.
6 σταυρῷ μετὰ τὸ μαστιχθῆναι προση-
λώθη.

4   **Ταύτῃ τῇ τιμῇ τιμήσωμεν**
κ.τ.λ.] "With this honour let us
honour" or "At this price let us
apprize, the Son of God." There is
perhaps a play upon the double
sense of τιμή and τιμᾶν For the
first we may compare (with Harnack) Acts xxviii. 10 πολλαῖς τιμαῖς

ἐτίμησαν ἡμᾶς, and the proverb in
John iv. 44, perhaps also 1 Pet. ii. 6,
7 ; for the second, Matt. xxvii. 9 τὴν
τιμὴν τοῦ τετιμημένου ὃν ἐτιμήσαντο
ἀπὸ υἱῶν Ἰσραήλ. St Matthew cites
Zech. xi 13 where the LXX. misses
the sense, but Aquila (Euseb *d e*
479) had ὑπερμεγεθὴς ἡ τιμὴ ἣν ἐτιμή-
θην ὑπὲρ αὐτῶν The double meaning
is recognised in Tertullian *Marc.* iv.
40 "pretium appretiati vel honora-
ti"; comp also Cyril *catech.* xiii. 10

6   **καὶ ἤνεγκον δύο κακούργους**
κ.τ.λ] The Crucifixion follows immediately upon the Mockery. Comp.
Luke xxiii. 32 ἤγοντο δὲ καὶ ἕτεροι
κακοῦργοι δύο.   *Constitutions*, v. 14
δύο κακούργους ἐσταύρωσαν σὺν αὐτῷ.
Ev Nicod i (A) 10 ἅμα δὲ καὶ τοὺς δύο
κακούργους ἐκρέμασαν. In the N. T
κακοῦργος is used only by St Luke
and St Paul (2 Tim. ii 9) ; but St Peter
has κακοποιός four times Ἐσταύρωσαν
ἀνὰ μέσον αὐτῶν τὸν κύριον comes nearest to John xix 18 μέσον δὲ τὸν Ἰησοῦν
Cf Matt xiii 25 ; Mk. vii. 31

7.   **αὐτὸς δὲ ἐσιώπα, ὡς μηδὲν πόνον
ἔχων**] Comp. Matt xxvi. 63 ὁ δὲ Ἰησοῦς
ἐσιώπα. The silence of Christ before
His judges becomes in Peter a
silence at the moment of crucifixion
Peter omits (with ℵᵃBD*) the first
of the words on the Cross, although
it seems to have belonged (W. H.
app. 67 f.) to the 'western' text, and
stood (further on) in the Diatessaron.
It would not have been in keeping

πόνον ἔχων. καὶ ὅτε ὤρθωσαν τὸν σταυρόν, ἐπέγραψαν ὅτι Οὗτός ἐϲτιν ὁ Βαϲιλεὺϲ τοῦ Ἰϲραήλ καὶ τεθεικότες
τὰ ἐνδύματα ἔμπροσθεν αὐτοῦ διεμερίσαντο, καὶ λαχμὸν

1 πόνου Z | ο[...] | σαν : οτι εωρθωσαν B. : ὅτε ὤρθ. R, H, L., Z. | τον
σταυρων 2 [βασιλευς] 3 εμπ[ροσθεν]

with his anti-Judaic position. But
he has another reason for the exci-
sion, which is betrayed by his comment on the Lord's silence The
death of the Son of God must be
painless; that it was so, is indicated by His silence. Mr Rendel
Harris points out to me that the
Curetonian Syriac in Luke xxiii. 9
explained οὐδὲν ἀπεκρίνατο by adding
"as if He were not there", comp
Cod. Colbert. (c) "quasi non audiens."
The comparison is instructive, in
Peter the gloss is less innocent. Yet
Peter's Docetism is so guarded that
Origen is able to use similar words
in a Catholic sense : Matt. 125 "unigenita uirtus nocita non est sicut nec
passa est aliquid "
For πόνος 'pain,' cf. Gen. xxxiv 25,
Isa liii. 4, Apoc xvi. 10, 11, xxi 4 ,
and for the construction μηδὲν κτλ.
see Apoc iii 17 οὐδὲν χρείαν ἔχω—a
reference which I owe to Mr Murray.
  1. ὅτε ὤρθωσαν τὸν σταυρόν] A
detail not in the canonical Gospels,
although implied in their account of
the bearing of the Cross to the place
of execution cf. also John iii. 14,
viii 28, &c. It does not appear
whether Peter regards the Crucified
as lifted together with the Cross, or
attached to it after the elevation; see
Justus Lipsius de cruce, p. 82 ff. (ed.
1685). Ἐώρθωσαν, if sound, is formed
on the analogy of ἐώθουν, ἑώρακα, &c ,
but the ε cannot be detected in the
heliographic reproduction of the MS.
  2. Οὗτός ἐστιν ὁ βασιλεὺς τοῦ Ἰσ-
ραήλ] Mt , Οὗτός ἐστιν Ἰησοῦς ὁ β. τῶν
Ἰουδαίων Mk , Ὁ β. τῶν Ἰουδαίων. L.,
Ὁ β. τῶν Ἰουδαίων οὗτος. J , Ἰησοῦς ὁ
Ναζωραῖος ὁ β. τῶν Ἰουδαίων. Peter's

ἐπιγραφή comes nearest to St Luke's,
but differs from all in substituting τοῦ
Ἰσραήλ for τῶν Ἰουδ. The title is
regarded as the work of the Jews
(ἐπέγραψαν), not of Pilate ; and the
change is consistent with its assumed
origin In Matt. xxvii. 42, Mark xv.
32, the Jews under the Cross speak
derisively of " the King of Israel."
  3. τὰ ἐνδύματα διεμερίσαντο κ.τ.λ.]
Ps. xxi (xxii.) 19 διεμερίσαντο τὰ ἱμάτιά μου ἑαυτοῖς, καὶ ἐπὶ τὸν ἱματισμόν
μου ἔβαλον κλῆρον. The words are
quoted by St John (xix. 24), and
occur with slight variations in each
of the Synoptic Gospels. Peter,
after his manner, changes something
—ἱμάτια gives place to ἐνδύματα. In
common with Mt., Mk , L , he does
not distinguish between the ἱμάτια and
the ἱματισμός of the second member of
the parallelism, which St John identifies with the χιτών The distinction
is ignored by Justin also, although
the latter quotes the Psalm, and
seems to allude to St John. (See
next note.)
  καὶ λαχμὸν ἔβαλον ἐπ' αὐτοῖς] Comp.
Justin, dial 97 οἱ σταυρώσαντες
αὐτὸν ἐμέρισαν τὰ ἱμάτια αὐτοῦ ἑαυτοῖς,
λαχμὸν βάλλοντες ἕκαστος κατὰ
τὴν τοῦ κλήρου ἐπιβολήν, ὃ ἐκλέξασθαι
ἐβεβούλητο. Cyril of Jerusalem, catech
xiii. 26 οἱ στρατιῶται διεμερίσαντο
τὸ περιβόλαιον . . ὁ δὲ χιτὼν οὐκ
ἐσχίσθη . . καὶ λαχμὸς περὶ τούτου
γίνεται τοῖς στρατιώταις. καὶ τὸ μὲν
μερίζονται, περὶ τούτου δὲ λαγχάνουσιν.
ἆρα καὶ τοῦτο γέγραπται, . . διεμερίσαντο κτλ. (Ps. xxi. l. c.) . .
κλῆρος δὲ ἦν ὁ λαχμός. Cf. Etymol.
magn 519 10 κλῆρος .. σημαίνει .. ψή-
φους τινὰς ἐν αἷς ἐσημειοῦντο καὶ

ἔβαλον ἐπ᾽ αὐτοῖς. εἶς δέ τις τῶν κακούργων ἐκείνων ὠνείδισεν αὐτοὺς λέγων ʽΗμεῖς διὰ τὰ κακὰ ἃ ἐποιήσαμεν οὕτω πεπόνθαμεν· οὗτος δὲ σωτὴρ γενόμενος τῶν ἀνθρώπων τί ἠδίκησεν ὑμᾶς; καὶ ἀγανακτήσαντες 5 ἐπ᾽ αὐτῷ ἐκέλευσαν ἵνα μὴ σκελοκοπηθῇ, ὅπως βασανιζόμενος ἀποθάνοι.

V. ʼΗν δὲ μεσημβρία, καὶ σκότος κατέσχε πᾶσαν

1 [αυτοις]   2 ωνειδησεν   3 οὗτος] ουτως   6 ἀποθάνῃ H.

ἔγραφον τὰ ὀνόματα αὐτῶν, ὅπερ καὶ λαχμὸς λέγεται The lexx notice but one other instance of this use of λαχμός in Christian literature (Joseph. *hypomnest.* ap. Fabric *pseudepigr.* V. T 144 ἢ διὰ κλήρων...ἢ διὰ λαχμῶν); but add Nonn *paraphr.* p 202 λαχμῷ πάντες ἴδοιμεν ἀδηρίτῳ τίνος ἔσται (J M.C , *Scottish Guardian*, March 10) It should be observed that Symmachus translated יַפִּילוּ גוֹרָל in the Ps by ἐλάγχανον, and that St John represents the soldiers as saying in reference to the χιτών, Λάχωμεν περὶ αὐτοῦ.

1. **εἶς δέ τις τῶν κακούργων κ τ.λ.**] St Luke begins nearly in the same way εἶς δὲ τῶν κρεμασθέντων κακούργων. But Peter's treatment of the incident is widely different He ignores the impenitent malefactor , he omits the conversation between the penitent and our Lord, and he represents the penitent's reproof as falling not on his comrade, but on the Jews The speech is clearly an imitation of Luke xxiii 40, 41 ἡμεῖς μὲν δικαίως, ἄξια γὰρ ὧν ἐπράξαμεν ἀπολαμβάνομεν· οὗτος δὲ οὐδὲν ἄτοπον ἔπραξεν . cf. Matt xxvii 23 τί γὰρ κακὸν ἐποίησεν; In σωτὴρ γενόμενος we have an echo of St Luke's σῶσον σεαυτον καὶ ἡμᾶς (*v.* 39). But the writer borrows also from Mt. and Mk. ; ὠνείδισεν αὐτούς is from Matt. xxvii. 44, Mark xv. 32, and

ἵνα μὴ σκελοκοπηθῇ, while it contradicts a statement of St John, is probably based upon it . see next note.

5 **ἵνα μὴ σκελοκοπηθῇ κ τ λ**] The *crurifragium* was, it seems, employed in crucifixions among the Jews in order to comply with the law of Deut. xxi Comp John xix. 31, 32, where an exception is made only in the case of our Lord, because He was already dead (J Lipsius, p. 109). To have abandoned it in this case would have been to bring about the very infringement of the Law which Petei represents the Jews as anxious to prevent Either he has overlooked this point, or he means to suggest that their conduct was as shortsighted as it was cruel In any case he looks upon the *crurifragium* of the crucified as an act of mercy, and this, it has been observed, is regarded by Origen also as one if not the more probable of two alternative aspects of the practice : *Matth.* 140 "miserti sunt ergo Judaei . aut forte non propter misericordiam hoc fecerunt...sed principaliter propter sabbatum"; cf. Nonnus *ad loc.* Σκελοκοπεῖν is unknown to the lexicons, but there are exx of σκελοκοπία.

7. **ἦν δὲ μεσημβρία**] Mt., ἀπὸ δὲ ἔκτης ὥρας. Mk., καὶ γενομένης ὥρας ἔκτης· L, καὶ ἦν ἤδη ὡσεὶ ὥρα ἔκτη. Μεσημβρία in this sense occurs in

8 ΕΥΑΓΓΕΛΙΟΝ ΚΑΤΑ ΠΕΤΡΟΝ

τὴν Ἰουδαίαν· καὶ ἐθορυβοῦντο καὶ ἠγωνίων μή ποτε ὁ
ἥλιος ἔδυ, ἐπειδὴ ἔτι ἔζη· γέγραπται αὐτοῖς ἥλιον
μὴ δῦναι ἐπὶ πεφονευμένῳ. καί τις αὐτῶν εἶπεν

3 πεφωνευμενω

the N. T. only in Acts xxii. 6. In
the LXX. it is common, and the word
is possibly preferred by Peter on
account of its use in Amos viii.
9 δύσεται ὁ ἥλιος μεσημβρίας καὶ συσκο-
τάσει ἐπὶ τῆς γῆς ἐν ἡμέρᾳ τὸ φῶς, a
passage which is interpreted as a
prophecy of the Three hours' darkness by Euseb. *dem. ev.* p. 486, Cyril of
Jerusalem *catech* xiii. 25, and Cyril
of Alexandria, *ad loc.*
σκότος κατέσχε πᾶσαν τὴν Ἰουδαίαν]
Mt, σκότος ἐγένετο ἐπὶ πᾶσαν τὴν γῆν
(Mk., L., ἐφ' ὅλην τὴν γῆν). For
σκότος κατέσχε cf. 2 Kings i. 9 κατ-
έσχεν με σκότος δεινόν: Origen
Matt. 134 interprets τὴν γῆν with the
same reservation· "tenebrae tantum-
modo super omnem terram Iudaeam
sunt factae." Comp Ciasca, *Tatian,*
p. 92 "tenebrae occupaverunt uni-
versam terram."
I. ἐθορυβοῦντο καὶ ἠγωνίων] For θορυ-
βεῖσθαι in this sense comp Mark v.
39 τί θορυβεῖσθε καὶ κλαίετε; Ἀγω-
νιᾷν is a form unknown to the N T.,
but common in Polybius, e.g. 2. 6. 8,
5. 34. 9; in Dan. i 10 LXX. ἀγωνιῶ
=φοβοῦμαι Theod. The fear was
that the sun had already set; for He
was yet alive, and the Law would be
broken by the Crucified remaining
on the Cross after sunset. The
repetition of the words γέγραπται κ τ λ.
without a connecting γάρ has suggested the idea that in this place
they have been brought in from the
margin and were not part of the
original text. In any case Peter
adheres to the interpretation of Deut.
xxi. 23 which he has given above
(c. ii.).

3. καί τις αὐτῶν εἶπεν κ.τ λ.] Mt., εἰς
ἐξ αὐτῶν The best course was now to
hasten the death, and it is apparently
with this intention that the draught
which Peter describes is administered.
Origen *Matt.* 137 may have had
this in view when he compares the
sponge to the writings of unbelievers
filled "non de uerbo potabili neque
de uino laetificante cor hominis neque de aqua refectionis, sed de aliquo
contrario et nociuo et non potabili
aceto intelligibili." Nonnus modifies
this view of the incident by ascribing
the intention to our Lord νοήσας |
ὅττι θοῶς τετέλεστο, θοώτερον ἤθελεν
εἶναι Peter's account depends here
not upon the Gospels, but upon Ps
lxviii (=lxix) 22 καὶ ἔδωκαν εἰς τὸ
βρῶμά μου χολήν, καὶ εἰς τὴν δίψαν μου
ἐπότισάν με ὄξος (comp. Origen *l. c.*
"sic impleuit prophetiam") The
Psalm is not directly quoted by any
of the Evangelists, and the χολή is
mentioned only in Matt. xxvii. 34,
which refers to the draught offered
to our Lord before the Crucifixion,
and not to that which was administered just before His death : ἔδωκαν
αὐτῷ πιεῖν οἶνον (*v. l.* ὄξος) μετὰ
χολῆς μεμιγμένον. The combination
ὄξος μετὰ χολῆς is not unusual (e g.
Constitutions, v. 14 ἔδωκαν αὐτῷ ὄξος
πιεῖν μετὰ χολῆς. cf. *Ev. Nicod.* 1.
(A) 16; for the form suggested by
the Psalm compare Barnabas 7 μέλλετε ποτίζειν χολὴν μετὰ ὄξους: *Orac.
Sibyll* viii. 303 ἐς δὲ τὸ βρῶμα χολὴν
καὶ πίεμεν ὄξος ἔδωκαν. *Ev. Nicod.* 1.
(B) 10 λαβὼν σπόγγον καὶ πλήσας αὐτὸν
χολῆς καὶ ὄξους. Cyril, who follows
Peter in citing the Psalm in this

Ποτίσατε αὐτὸν χολὴν μετὰ ὄξους· καὶ κεράσαντες
ἐπότισαν. καὶ ἐπλήρωσαν πάντα, καὶ ἐτελείωσαν
κατὰ τῆς κεφαλῆς αὐτῶν τὰ ἁμαρτήματα. περιήρχοντο δὲ πολλοὶ μετὰ λύχνων, νομίζοντες ὅτι νύξ
5 ἐστιν· [τινὲς δὲ] ἐπέσαντο. καὶ ὁ κύριος ἀνεβόησε

1 ποτίσατε αὐτὸν χολὴν obscure 5—6 νύξ ἐστιν...ἐπέσαντο] ἐπέσαντο may
have been re-written. the scribe seems to have begun νυξεστινεσ.. R., L., Z.
read ἔπεσάν τε, H. prefers [καὶ] ἐπέσαντο: Redpath conjectures ἐξίσταντο.

connexion, explains χολή as referring to Mark xv. 23 (catech. xiii
29 χολώδης δὲ καὶ κατάπικρος ἡ σμύρνα). With ποτίσατε.. χολήν comp.
Jer. viii. 14 ἐπότισεν ἡμᾶς ὕδωρ χολῆς,
ix. 15 ποτιῶ αὐτοὺς ὕδωρ χολῆς.

2. καὶ ἐπλήρωσαν πάντα κ τ.λ.] This
fulfilment of Psalm lxix completed the
accomplishment of the Passion-pro-
phecies. The reference is perhaps to
John xix. 28 ff. ἵνα τελειωθῇ ἡ γραφὴ
λέγει Διψῶ .. ὅτε οὖν ἔλαβεν τὸ ὄξος ὁ
Ἰησοῦς εἶπεν Τετέλεσται (consummata
sunt omnia in the Arabic Diatessaron; cf. 28 πάντα τετέλεσται). St
John uses πληροῦν of the fulfilment
of Scripture in the same context (xix
24, 36). With ἐτελείωσαν.. τὰ ἁμαρτήματα comp. Gen xv. 16 οὔπω ἀνα-
πεπλήρωνται αἱ ἁμαρτίαι. Matt. xxiii
32 πληρώσατε τὸ μέτρον. 1 Thess ii. 16
εἰς τὸ ἀναπληρῶσαι αὐτῶν τὰς ἁμαρτίας.
See Barn. xiv. 5 ἵνα κἀκεῖνοι τελειω-
θῶσιν τοῖς ἁμαρτήμασιν. Didasc. v. 17
ἐτέλεσαν τὴν πονηρίαν αὐτῶν Κατὰ
τῆς κεφαλῆς probably refers to Matt.
xxvii. 25 ἐφ᾽ ἡμᾶς cf. Acts xviii. 6,
and for the exact phrase 1 Cor.
xi. 4.

3. περιήρχοντο δὲ πολλοὶ μετὰ λύχνων κ.τ.λ.] Anaph. Pilati (B) 7 ἐν
παντὶ τῷ κόσμῳ ἦψαν λύχνους ἀπὸ
ἕκτης ὥρας ἕως ὀψίας With νομίζοντες ὅτι νύξ ἐστιν compare Orac.
Sibyll. viii. 305—6 ἤματι μέσσῳ | νὺξ
ἔσται σκοτόεσσα: Didasc. v. 14 ἔπειτα
ἐγένετο τρεῖς ὥρας σκότος καὶ ἐλογίσθη
νύξ. Euseb d e. p 487 ἡμέρας οὔσης
νὺξ ἀπὸ ὥρας ἕκτης τὸ περιέχον συν-

ἔσχε μέχρι τῆς ἐνάτης. Cyril. catech.
xiii. 24 σκότος ἐγένετο ἐν ἡμέρᾳ μέσῃ
... ὠνόμασε δὲ ὁ θεὸς τὸ σκότος νύκτα.
The Didascalia reveals a motive for
the stress laid upon the night-like
character of the darkness; if the
three hours were counted as a night,
it was possible to maintain the literal
accuracy of Matt. xii. 40. Reference
is also made to Amos viii. 9, Zech.
xiv. 6, 7. Ἐπέσαντο has caused much
difficulty. Prof Robinson at once
suggested a reference to John xviii.
6 and to Isaiah lix. 10 πεσοῦνται ἐν
μεσημβρίᾳ, and if the word is sound,
the latter passage is almost certainly
in view. See however the critical
note.

5. ὁ κύριος ἀνεβόησε κ.τ.λ.] The
silence is broken at length by a loud
cry Matt. xxvii 46 ἀνεβόησεν (ἐβόησεν BL, 33, al, so Mk.) ὁ Ἰησοῦς
φωνῇ μεγάλῃ. The words of the
cry in the Petrine fragment depart
widely from those in Mt. and Mk., as
well as from the original; ὁ θεός (= θεέ
Mk.) becomes ἡ δύναμις, the second
μου and ἵνα τί (εἰς τί Mk.) disappear,
ἐγκατέλιπες is replaced by κατέλειψας
(cf Acts vi. 3). The variants of
the LXX. throw no light on any of
these changes, nor is the Fourth
Word cited in any but the canonical
form by the great writers of the
second and third centuries. Eusebius indeed throws light on the
substitution of δύναμις for θεός; after
remarking (dem. ev. p. 494) that the
Heb. has יִלֵא and not יהלֶא he points

λέγων Ἡ Δύναμίς Μογ, ἡ Δύναμιc, κατέλειψάc με· καὶ εἰπὼν ἀνελήφθη. καὶ αὐτῆς [τῆς] ὥρας διεράγη τὸ καταπέτασμα τοῦ ναοῦ τῆς Ἰερουσαλὴμ εἰς δύο.

2 αὐτῆς τῆς ὥρας] αυτος ωρας· αὐτῆς τῆς ὤ. R., H., Z., αὐτῆς ὥρας L

out that Aquila alone recognised the distinction: οὐκ ἠξίωσεν ὁμοίως τοῖς λοιποῖς ὁ θεὸς ὁ θεός Μογ μεταβαλὼν εἰπεῖν, ἀλλά Ἰcχγρέ Μογ Ἰcχγρέ Μογ —adding τὸ δὲ ἀκριβές ἐστιν Ἰcχγ́c Μογ Ἰcχγ́c Μογ. The Lord, Eusebius adds, would not have died, unless His Strong One (i.e. the Father) had left Him καταλέλοιπεν οὖν αὐτὸν ὁ Ἰσχυρὸς αὐτοῦ, θελήσας αὐτὸν μέχρι θανάτου. κατελθεῖν. For אל = δύναμις comp Justin, dial. 125 τὸ οὖν Ἰσραὴλ ὄνομα τοῦτο σημαίνει "Ἀνθρωπος νικῶν δύναμιν· τὸ γὰρ Ἰσρά ἄνθρωπος νικῶν ἐστι, τὸ δὲ ἤλ δύναμις: and the O. T. phrase לאל יְדִי (אין)-יֶשׁ (Gen. xxxi 29, Prov. iii. 27, Mic ii. 1, Neh. v. 5 where the LXX. has οὐκ ἔστιν δύναμις χειρὸς ἡμῶν). But אל may have been confused with חֵיל, and if so, Aquila's ἰσχύς was, as Eusebius says, ἀκριβές: δύναμις is the LXX. rendering of חֵיל in about 150 places. Cf. Theodoret haer fabb v. 4 τὸ δὲ ηλ ψιλούμενον μὲν καὶ αὐτὸ δηλοῖ τὸν θεόν, δασυνόμενον δὲ τὸν ἰσχυρόν More remarkable is Peter's conversion of the question into a direct statement by the omission of ἵνα τί. I can produce only one parallel Ephraim tells us (serm adv. haer. 56) that at the assemblies of a Gnostic sect which he connects with the name of Bardaisan a hymn was sung in which a female voice recited the words ܐܠܗܝ ܘܪܝܫܝ ܫܒܩܬܢܝ ܒܠܚܘܕܝ "My God and my Head, thou hast left me alone."

(I owe the ref. to D. C. B. I. 253.) A Valentinian party mentioned by Irenaeus (i 8. 2) taught that the Lord ἐν μὲν τῷ εἰπεῖν 'Ο θεός μου [Lat. Deus meus Deus meus] εἰς τί ἐγκατέλιπές με, μεμηνυκέναι ὅτι ἀπελείφθη ἀπὸ τοῦ φωτὸς ἡ Σοφία καὶ ἐκωλύθη ὑπὸ τοῦ "Ορου τῆς εἰς τοὔμπροσθεν ὁρμῆς But the original form of the word is here retained

1 καὶ εἰπὼν ἀνελήφθη] Comp. 'Mark' xvi. 19 ὁ μὲν οὖν κύριος μετὰ τὸ λαλῆσαι αὐτοῖς ἀνελήμφθη. Peter removes the ἀνάλημψις to the moment of death, and the expression has been adopted by Origen Matt. 140 "statim ut clamavit ad Patrem receptus est. post tres horas receptus est", the Greek is lost, but receptus est is the O. L. rendering of ἀνελήμφθη in Irenaeus and in the Munich Gospels known as q (White, p. 137). With Peter's view of this ἀνάλημψις comp Clem. Alex. exc. Theod. § 61 ἀπέθανεν δὲ ἀποστάντος τοῦ καταβάντος ἐπ' αὐτῷ ἐπὶ τῷ Ἰορδάνῃ πνεύματος.

2 διεράγη τὸ καταπέτασμα κτλ] Cyril catech. xiii. 32 τὸ καταπέτασμα τοῦ ναοῦ .. διερρήξατο. Ib. 39 τὸ τότε διαρραγέν. Jerome in Matt. xxvii. "in euangelio cuius saepe facimus mentionem [eu. sec. Hebraeos] superliminare templi infinitae magnitudinis fractum esse atque diuisum legimus" Τῆς Ἰερουσαλήμ is one of several indications that the fragment was written outside Palestine, or at all events for non-Palestinian readers.

VI. Καὶ τότε ἀπέσπασαν τοὺς ἥλους ἀπὸ τῶν
χειρῶν τοῦ κυρίου, καὶ ἔθηκαν αὐτὸν ἐπὶ τῆς γῆς· καὶ
ἡ γῆ πᾶσα ἐσείσθη καὶ φόβος μέγας ἐγένετο. τότε
ἥλιος ἔλαμψε καὶ εὑρέθη ὥρα ἐνάτη. ἐχάρησαν δὲ οἱ
5 Ἰουδαῖοι καὶ δεδώκασι τῷ Ἰωσὴφ τὸ σῶμα αὐτοῦ ἵνα
αὐτὸ θάψῃ, ἐπειδὴ θεασάμενος ἦν ὅσα ἀγαθὰ ἐποίησεν.

3 ἐγένετο] 1ª m. εγενετε   5 ινι

1. καὶ τότε ἀπέσπασαν τοὺς ἥλους
κτλ.] With καὶ τότε comp c 1.
The Fourth Gospel alone mentions
the ἥλοι and, like Peter, mentions
them only in connexion with the
Hands   So Cyril *catech* xiii 28
ἐξέτεινεν ἀνθρωπίνας χεῖρας καὶ προσεπάγησαν ἥλοις. On the other hand
Justin, referring to Ps xxi (xxii) 17,
writes (*dial* 97) ἐσταύρωσαν αὐτὸν
ἐμπήσσοντες τοὺς ἥλους τὰς χεῖρας καὶ
τοὺς πόδας αὐτοῦ ὤρυξαν *infra*, πόδας
καὶ χεῖρας ὠρύγη.
2 ἔθηκαν . ἐσείσθη] 'When the
Lord's Body was laid upon the earth,
the whole earth quaked.' The incident is mentioned only by St
Matthew (xxvii. 51), who however
connects it with the Death, and not
with the preparation for Burial.
Πᾶσα (which is not in Matt) suggests
a reference to Jer viii. 16 ἐσείσθη
πᾶσα ἡ γῆ. comp *Ev Nicod* 1 (B) 11
σεισμὸς γὰρ ἐγένετο ἐπὶ τὴν γῆν ἅπασαν
3. καὶ φόβος μέγας ἐγένετο] Matt.
xxvii. 54 ὁ δὲ ἑκατόνταρχος καὶ οἱ μετ᾽
αὐτοῦ . . ἰδόντες τὸν σεισμὸν καὶ τὰ
γινόμενα ἐφοβήθησαν σφόδρα
τότε ἥλιος ἔλαμψε κτλ.] Cyril
catech xiii. 24 μετὰ τὴν ἐνάτην ἔλαμψεν
ὁ ἥλιος· προλέγει καὶ τοῦτο ὁ προφήτης (Zech. xiv. 7) Καὶ πρὸς ἑσπέραν
ἔσται φῶς. Ephraim, *evang concord*
exp. p. 257 "tres horas sol obtene-
bratus est et postea denuo luxit."
Once more the *gnomon* shewed the
hour, and it was seen to be (εὑρέθη)
3 p m. The fact came to the Jews

with the force of a discovery, so
impressed had they been with the
belief that it was night
4. ἐχάρησαν δὲ οἱ Ἰουδαῖοι κτλ]
The Jewish leaders rejoiced, whether
at the reappearance of the Sun, the
frustration of their fears that the
Law would be broken (c. v), or the
success of their murderous design;
if the last, comp John xvi. 21 ὁ δὲ
κόσμος χαρήσεται. In their joy they
place no difficulty in Joseph's way;
δεδώκασι implies that the power to
refuse was really in their hands, notwithstanding Herod's jurisdiction (cf
c. ii.), for the perfect, cf. c viii. (παραδέδωκεν). Ἐπειδὴ θεασάμενος .
ἐποίησεν must be taken as a jeer:
'Joseph had been a disciple, he had
witnessed all the good deeds of the
Crucified, let him bury the Body if
he would', unless we accept the sug-
gestion of Mr Nicholson (*Academy*,
Dec 17), that the words were originally a marginal note attached to
the story of the penitent thief, and
were afterwards shifted into the
margin of the present passage and
from thence into the text. But this
explanation seems unnecessary. In
their lightheartedness the Scribes
and Priests indulge themselves in
heartless banter at the expense of
Joseph The words appear to have
been suggested by John xi. 45 θεασάμενος ὃ (v. l. ἃ) ἐποίησεν· comp.
Acts ix. 36 ἦν πλήρης ἔργων ἀγαθῶν..ὧν
ἐποίει.

λαβὼν δὲ τὸν κύριον ἔλουσε καὶ εἵλησε σινδόνι καὶ
εἰσήγαγεν εἰς ἴδιον τάφον καλούμενον Κῆπον Ἰωσήφ.
VII. Τότε οἱ Ἰουδαῖοι καὶ οἱ πρεσβύτεροι καὶ οἱ
ἱερεῖς, γνόντες οἷον κακὸν ἑαυτοῖς ἐποίησαν, ἤρξαντο
κόπτεσθαι καὶ λέγειν Οὐαὶ ταῖς ἁμαρτίαις ἡμῶν· 5

1 εἵλησε] ἐνείλησε H., Z. | σινδονιν
εα]υτοις | [η]ρξ[α]ντο κοπτε[σ]θ[αι]

3 οἱ ἱερεῖς] οιερεις   4 [κακον

1. λαβὼν δὲ τὸν κύριον κ.τ.λ] Matt.
xxvii. 59 καὶ λαβὼν τὸ σῶμα, John xix.
40 ἔλαβον τὸ σῶμα. Comp. John xx.
2 ἦραν τὸν κύριον ἐκ τοῦ μνημείου.
For ἔλουσε see Acts ix. 37 λού-
σαντες δὲ ἔθηκαν ἐν ὑπερῴῳ. Εἵλησε
σινδόνι is from Mark xv. 46 ἐνείλησεν
τῇ σινδόνι : Mt., L., have ἐνετύλιξεν
[ἐν] σινδ., J. has ἔδησαν ὀθονίοις.

2. εἰσήγαγεν ... Κῆπον Ἰωσήφ]
Εθηκεν αὐτὸ[ν] (so all the Synoptists)
ἐν τῷ καινῷ αὐτοῦ μνημείῳ (Mk.) Τάφος
is used by Mt just afterwards (xxvii.
61, xxviii. 1). Ἦν δὲ (adds St John
xix. 41) ἐν τῷ τόπῳ ὅπου ἐσταυρώθη
κῆπος, καὶ ἐν τῷ κήπῳ μνημεῖον καινόν
ἐκεῖ οὖν...ὅτι ἐγγὺς ἦν τὸ μνημεῖον
ἔθηκαν Ἰησοῦν. In the Diatessaron
these words intervene between Mark
xv. 46 and Matt. xxvii 60   Peter's
κῆπος καλούμενος κ.τ.λ. may have
arisen simply from a desire to con-
vey the impression of independent
knowledge ; yet Harnack's question
should be kept in view · "war der
κῆπος Ἰ. zur Zeit des Verfassers etwa
eine bekannte Localitat?" Comp
Acts i 19 γνωστὸν ἐγένετο πᾶσι τοῖς
κατοικοῦσιν Ἰερουσαλήμ, ὥστε κληθῆναι
τὸ χωρίον ἐκεῖνο Χωρίον αἵματος.

3. τότε οἱ Ἰουδαῖοι κ.τ.λ] The
momentary joy is changed into general mourning, in which for different
reasons the Jewish leaders (c. vii),
the Disciples (ib.), and the whole
people (c viii.), take part.   There
is again a reference to prophecy :
comp Amos viii. 10 μεταστρέψω τὰς
ἑορτὰς ὑμῶν εἰς πένθος καὶ πάσας τὰς

ᾠδὰς ὑμῶν εἰς θρῆνον ὡς πένθος ἀγα-
πητοῦ. Eusebius (d e. p. 486) interprets Amos l.c in a wider sense ἐξ
ἐκείνου καὶ εἰς δεῦρο μετέστρεψεν αὐτῶν
ὁ θεὸς τὰς ἑορτὰς εἰς πένθος ..τῆς περι-
βοήτου μητροπόλεως ἀποστερήσας αὐτοὺς
κ.τ.λ. Cyril however (catech xiii 25)
follows Peter . ἐν ἀζύμοις γὰρ ἦν τὸ
πραχθὲν καὶ τῇ τοῦ πάσχα ἑορτῇ, and
proceeds to describe the grief of the
Apostles and the women. 'The
Jews' are the Elders and Priests:
cf c. viii οἱ γραμματεῖς καὶ Φαρισαῖοι
καὶ πρεσβύτεροι   infra, οἱ πρεσβ,
πρεσβ καὶ γραμματεῖς . comp. Matt.
xxvii. 41 οἱ ἀρχιερεῖς μετὰ τῶν γραμμα-
τέων καὶ πρεσβυτέρων, 62 οἱ ἀρχιερεῖς
καὶ οἱ Φαρισαῖοι, xxviii. 11 τοῖς ἀρχιε-
ρεῦσιν...μετὰ τῶν πρεσβυτέρων

4. ἤρξαντο κόπτεσθαι καὶ λέγειν Οὐαὶ
κ.τ λ.] The words attributed to the
leaders are substantially those which
are put into the mouth of the ὄχλοι
in some early versions of Luke xxiii
48 . the Curetonian Syriac inserts
there ܘܐ . ܐܡ ܪ̈ܝܫ ܠ ܗ

ܠ ܗ ܦ ܝܨ̈ܘ (comp. the Doctrine
of Addai, Cureton, Ancient Syriac
Documents, pp. 9, 10), and in a fuller
form, closely akin to that which seems
to have been known to Peter, they
occur in the O.L. cod. Sangerman-
ensis (g1) "uae nobis quae facta sunt
hodie propter peccata nostra, appro-
pinquauit enim desolatio Hierusa-
lem." That the words in some form
stood in the text of Tatian is
probable from Ephraim's comment

ἤγγισεν ἡ κρίσις καὶ τὸ τέλος Ἰερουσαλήμ. ἐγὼ δὲ
μετὰ τῶν ἑταίρων μου ἐλυπούμην, καὶ τετρωμένοι κατὰ
διάνοιαν ἐκρυβόμεθα· ἐζητούμεθα γὰρ ὑπ' αὐτῶν ὡς
κακοῦργοι καὶ ὡς τὸν ναὸν θέλοντες ἐμπρῆσαι· ἐπὶ δὲ
5 τούτοις πᾶσιν ἐνηστεύομεν, καὶ ἐκαθεζόμεθα πενθοῦντες
καὶ κλαίοντες νυκτὸς καὶ ἡμέρας ἕως τοῦ σαββάτου.

2—3 κ[ατα δια]νοιαν   4 ε[μπρησαι]   5 εκα[θεζομε]θα

ev. conc. p. 248 "quia uox prima ludi-
brium erat in ore eorum uox altera
Uae facta est in ore eorum et complosio
manuum in pectore eorum", further
on E refers to the prophets who
'foretold the destruction of their city'
(cf. *infra*, p. 252)   The genesis of
the interpolation is hardly doubtful
Οὐαί is the natural accompaniment
of κοπετός, comp 3 Kings xiii 30
ἐκόψαντο αὐτόν Οὐαὶ ἀδελφέ, and
would soon assert its right to follow
τύπτοντες τὰ στήθη Or it may have
alluded to a prophetic *locus classicus,*
Cyril. *catech* xiii. 12 refers to Isa iii.
9 οὐαὶ τῇ ψυχῇ αὐτῶν ὅτι βεβούλευνται
βουλὴν πονηρὰν καθ' ἑαυτῶν (cf p. 12,l 4).
The next step would be to add the
words ἤγγισεν ἡ κρίσις or ἡ ἐρήμωσις
or τὸ τέλος Ἰερουσαλήμ, or some combination of them founded on Dan. ix
2, 26 or on Luke xxi. 20 (comp Apoc.
xviii. 10, 19 οὐαὶ οὐαὶ ἡ πόλις ἡ μεγάλη
...ἦλθεν ἡ κρίσις σου ἠρημώθη). Such
words would have acquired a special
force in reference to Jerusalem at the
time of the final crushing out of the
Jewish national life under Hadrian.

1 ἐγὼ δὲ μετὰ τῶν ἑταίρων κ τ λ]
The personal character of the narrative appears here; cf. *infra*, c. xii.
ἐγὼ Σίμων Πέτρος. Comp *Constitutions* ii. 46, iv. 7, v. 7, vi. 12, vii. 11.
Ἑταῖρος is not used in the N. T. as=
συμμαθητής (John xi 16) With ἐλυπούμην comp John xvi 20 and Pet.
xii.   Τετρωμένοι κατὰ διάνοιαν,
again, is not in the style of the
N.T., but a similar phrase occurs in

2 Macc. iii. 16; comp Diod. Sic. 17.
112 οἱονεὶ τετρωμένος τὴν ψυχήν.   Ἐ-
κρυβόμεθα may have been suggested by
John viii. 59, xii. 36 (cf. xix. 38), or by
the incident of John xx 19; it is
copied by Cyril. *catech* xiii. 25 ὠδυνῶντο δὲ ἀποκρυβέντες οἱ ἀπόστολοι.
3 ἐζητούμεθα γὰρ κ.τ λ.] Comp.
Matt. xxii 7 ἀπώλεσεν τοὺς φονεῖς
ἐκείνους καὶ τὴν πόλιν αὐτῶν ἐνέπρησεν.
Ephraim *l.c.* "sanctuarium combus-
tum et templum dirutum est." That
the Apostles had designs upon the
Temple might well have been inferred
from the language attributed to the
Master (Mark xiv. 58, xv. 29; cf.
Acts vi. 13, 14).

4 ἐπὶ δὲ τούτοις πᾶσιν ἐνη-
στεύομεν] 'To add to our troubles we
were keeping fast' Mark ii 20 ἐλεύ-
σονται δὲ ἡμέραι ὅταν ἀπαρθῇ ἀπ' αὐτῶν
ὁ νυμφίος καὶ τότε νηστεύσουσιν ἐν
ἐκείνῃ τῇ ἡμέρᾳ (L, ἐν ἐκείναις ταῖς
ἡμέραις). *Constit* v. 19 ἡμεῖς ἐνηστεύσαμεν ἐν τῷ ἀναλημφθῆναι αὐτὸν
ἀφ' ἡμῶν. The *Didascalia* (v. 14)
represents the Paschal meal as having
been eaten on Tuesday evening (τῇ
γὰρ τρίτῃ ἑσπέρας σὺν ὑμῖν τὸ πάσχα
ἔφαγον), and followed the same night
by the arrest, after which the Lord is
kept in ward for two days before the
Crucifixion. If this was Peter's view,
the third day of the fast had already
come.

5. ἐκαθεζόμεθα πενθ. καὶ κλαίοντες
κτλ] Neh. i. 4 ἐκάθισα καὶ ἔκλαυσα
καὶ ἐπένθησα ἡμέρας καὶ ἤμην νηστεύων.
Ps. cxxxvi (cxxxvii) 1 ἐκαθίσαμεν

VIII. Συναχθέντες δὲ οἱ γραμματεῖς καὶ Φαρισαῖοι καὶ πρεσβύτεροι πρὸς ἀλλήλους, ἀκούσαντες ὅτι ὁ λαὸς ἅπας γογγύζει καὶ κόπτεται τὰ στήθη λέγοντες ὅτι Εἰ τῷ θανάτῳ αὐτοῦ ταῦτα τὰ μέγιστα σημεῖα γέγονεν, ἴδετε ὅτι πόσον δίκαιός ἐστιν· ἐφοβήθησαν οἱ 5 πρεσβύτεροι, καὶ ἦλθον πρὸς Πειλᾶτον δεόμενοι αὐτοῦ καὶ λέγοντες Παράδος ἡμῖν στρατιώτας, ἵνα φυλάξω[μεν] τὸ μνῆμα αὐτοῦ ἐπὶ τρεῖς ἡμέρας, μή ποτε ἐλθόντες οἱ μαθηταὶ αὐτοῦ κλέψωσιν αὐτὸν καὶ ὑπολάβῃ ὁ λαὸς ὅτι ἐκ νεκρῶν ἀνέστη, καὶ ποιήσωσιν ἡμῖν κακά. ὁ δὲ 10

5 ὅτι πόσον] ὁποσον H, Z.   7 φυλαξω   φυλάξω[σι] R, Z, φυλάξω[μεν]
H, L.   8 ημ[ερας]

καὶ ἐκλαύσαμεν. Thren. 1. 1 ἐκάθισεν Ἰερεμίας κλαίων καὶ ἐθρήνησεν John XI. 20 ἐν τῷ οἴκῳ ἐκαθέζετο. The order πενθεῖν καὶ κλαίειν occurs in Mark XVI. 10, James iv. 9.   Ἕως τοῦ σαββάτου may refer to the Paschal Sabbath which was now at hand, or possibly to the Sabbath of Easter week (infra, c XII.), in the former case νυκτὸς καὶ ἡμέρας looks back to the interval between the arrest and the night of Good Friday.

1. συναχθέντες δὲ ἦλθον πρὸς Πειλᾶτον] Matt. XXVII. 62 συνήχθησαν οἱ ἀρχιερεῖς καὶ οἱ Φαρισαῖοι πρὸς Πειλᾶτον (cf. XXVIII. 12). In Mt the gathering takes place on the Sabbath (τῇ...ἐπαύριον ἥτις ἐστὶν μετὰ τὴν παρασκευήν), and the party seem to go to Pilate without previous conference.   With συναχθ. πρὸς ἀλλήλους compare Acts IV 15 συνέβαλλον πρὸς ἀλλήλους.   Peter adds a new reason for these fears—the changed attitude of the populace.

3 ὁ λαὸς ἅπας γογγύζει καὶ κόπτεται τὰ στήθη κτλ] Luke XXIII 48 πάντες οἱ συνπαραγενόμενοι ὄχλοι ἐπὶ τὴν θεωρίαν ταύτην, θεωρήσαντες τὰ γενόμενα, τύπτοντες τὰ στήθη

ὑπέστρεφον   John VII 32 ἤκουσαν οἱ Φαρισαῖοι τοῦ ὄχλου γογγύζοντος περὶ αὐτοῦ ταῦτα.   Peter throws the γογγυσμός into words which combine L.'s version of the Centurion's confession (ὄντως ὁ ἄνθρωπος οὗτος δίκαιος ἦν) with a reference to the phaenomena that attended the Crucifixion (ταῦτα τὰ μέγιστα σημεῖα)   Κόπτεται τὰ στήθη mixes the two phrases κόπτεσθαί [τινα] (Luke XXIII 27) and τύπτειν τὰ στήθη   Ἴδετε ὅτι πόσον is a conflate of ἴδετε ὅτι and ἴδετε πόσον, whether due to the writer himself or to the copyists

7 στρατιώτας] The first mention in the fragment of the Roman soldiers. No part has been assigned to them either in the mockery or at the Crucifixion.   Mt. speaks here of a κουστωδία XXVII. 65, 66, but cf XXVIII. 13 τοῖς στρατιώταις.   Ἵνα φυλάξωμεν (? φυλάξωσι. MS, φυλάξω) κ.τ.λ   Comp. Mt κέλευσον οὖν ἀσφαλισθῆναι τὸν τάφον ἕως τῆς τρίτης ἡμέρας, μή ποτε ἐλθόντες οἱ μαθηταὶ [αὐτοῦ] κλέψωσιν αὐτὸν καὶ εἴπωσιν τῷ λαῷ Ἠγέρθη ἀπὸ τῶν νεκρῶν with ποιήσωσιν κακά, and supra (c. VII) οἷον κακὸν ἑαυτοῖς ἐποίησαν.

Πειλᾶτος παραδέδωκεν αὐτοῖς Πετρώνιον τὸν κεντυρίωνα
μετὰ στρατιωτῶν φυλάσσειν τὸν τάφον. καὶ σὺν
αὐτοῖς ἦλθον πρεσβύτεροι καὶ γραμματεῖς ἐπὶ τὸ μνῆμα,
καὶ κυλίσαντες λίθον μέγαν κατὰ τοῦ κεντυρίωνος καὶ
5 τῶν στρατιωτῶν ὁμοῦ πάντες οἱ ὄντες ἐκεῖ ἔθηκαν ἐπὶ
τῇ θύρᾳ τοῦ μνήματος, καὶ ἐπέχρισαν ἑπτὰ σφραγῖδας,

2 στρατιωτον   4 κατὰ] μετὰ R., H., L, Z.   6 επεχρεισαν

1. **Πετρώνιον τὸν κεντυρίωνα**] The
traditional name of the centurion
at the Cross was Longinus (*Ev.
Nicod.* 1 (B) 11 Λογγῖνος ὁ ἑκατόνταρχος ἱστάμενος εἶπεν Ἀληθῶς θεοῦ υἱὸς
ἦν οὗτος) A Spaniard named Oppius
is mentioned in the same connexion
by Dexter, *Chron* a 34 Peter, who
transfers the centurion to the Tomb,
finds another name for him Πετρώνιος, *Petronius*, is of frequent occur-
rence in inscriptions of the time of
the early Empire, and is familiar to
readers of Josephus (*Ant* xviii. 8
2, *B J.* 11 10) as the name of the
governor of Syria who was charged
by Caligula with the task of setting
up the Emperor's statue in the Temple But its use by Peter may have
been suggested by the similarity in
sound of Πετρώνιος and Πέτρος. Pe-
tronilla is the legendary name of St
Peter's daughter (Lightfoot, *Clement*,
i. 37). Peter writes κεντυρίων here
and *infra* (cc. ix., x) in preference to
ἑκατόνταρχος So St Mark (xv 39,
44, 45). cf *mart Polyc.* 18

2. **σὺν αὐτοῖς ἦλθον πρεσβύτεροι
κ.τ.λ.**] Matt. xxvii. 65 οἱ δὲ πορευθέντες
ἠσφαλίσαντο τὸν τάφον σφραγίσαντες
τὸν λίθον μετὰ τῆς κουστωδίας Peter
accentuates the cooperation of the
Jewish leaders ; *infra* (c ix.) παρῆσαν
γὰρ αὐτοὶ φυλάσσοντες   Μνῆμα
is St Luke's word (xxiii 53, xxiv. 1).

4. **κυλίσαντες λίθον μέγαν κ τ λ**]
In Mt., Mk. this is attributed to
Joseph (προσκυλίσας λίθον μέγαν τῇ

θύρᾳ τοῦ μνημείου ἀπῆλθεν = προσεκύ-
λισεν λίθον ἐπὶ τὴν θύραν τοῦ μνημείου)
But to roll to the door the great
stone (μέγας σφόδρα, Mark xvi. 4)
which was afterwards to be rolled
away by superhuman power, seemed
to need greater strength than that of
an individual, and Peter therefore
ascribes it to the combined efforts of
the members of the Sanhedrin and of
the guard (πάντες οἱ ὄντες ἐκεῖ). Comp.
the reading of D in Luke xxiii 53
ἐπέθηκεν τῷ μνημείῳ λίθον ὃν μόγις
εἴκοσι ἐκύλιον and the parallels in
Cod Colbert. (*quem vix viginti vol-
vebant*) and Theb. (J. R Harris,
Study of Codex Bezae, pp 47—
51)   Κατὰ τοῦ κ. καὶ τῶν στρ 'to
exclude the Centurion and soldiers,'
who might be bribed to deliver the
Body to the disciples The watch
of course are not cognisant of this
purpose

6. **ἐπέχρισαν ἑπτὰ σφραγῖδας**] Mt
simply σφραγίσαντες. For ἐπέχρισαν
comp John ix 6, 11 ἐπέχρισεν (BC*vid
ἐπέθηκεν) αὐτοῦ τὸν πηλὸν ἐπὶ τοὺς
ὀφθαλμούς : πηλὸν ἐποίησεν καὶ ἐπέχρισέν μου τοὺς ὀφθαλμούς Lucian
(πῶς δεῖ ἱστ. συγγρ. 62) ἐπιχρίσας
τιτάνῳ καὶ ἐπικαλύψας ἐπέγραψε
τοὔνομα τοῦ τότε βασιλεύοντος. For
the number of the seals comp. Acts
xii. 10 (D) κατέβησαν τοὺς ζ βαθμοὺς
and Apoc. v 1 βιβλίον...κατεσφρα-
γισμένον σφραγῖσιν ἑπτά. But Peter
may also have in view Zech. iii. 9 ἐπὶ
τὸν λίθον τὸν ἕνα ἑπτὰ ὀφθαλμοί

καὶ σκηνὴν ἐκεῖ πήξαντες ἐφύλαξαν. πρωΐας δέ, ἐπι-
φώσκοντος τοῦ σαββάτου, ἦλθεν ὄχλος ἀπὸ Ἰερουσαλὴμ καὶ τῆς περιχώρου ἵνα ἴδωσι τὸ μνημεῖον ἐσφρα-
γισμένον.
IX. Τῇ δὲ νυκτὶ ᾗ ἐπέφωσκεν ἡ κυριακή, φυλασ- 5
σόντων τῶν στρατιωτῶν ἀνὰ δύο δύο κατὰ φρουράν,

5 ηι

εἰσιν. IV. 10 ἑπτὰ οὗτοι ὀφθαλμοί εἰσιν
οἱ ἐπιβλέποντες ἐπὶ πᾶσαν τὴν γῆν. cf.
Apoc. v. 6 The 'seven seals'
not only constitute a perfect safe-
guard, but probably belong to the
symbolical teaching of the fragment.
1. σκηνὴν ἐκεῖ πήξαντες ἐφύλαξαν]
Matt. xvii. 4 ποιήσω ὧδε τρεῖς σκηνάς
(cf. Mk., L). Heb. viii. 2 σκηνῆς ἦν
ἔπηξεν ὁ κύριος.
πρωΐας δὲ κ.τ.λ.] The rumour that
the tomb was sealed and guarded
had reached the City and suburbs
during the night, and early on the
Sabbath morning crowds came to
see it. Comp. John xii. 9 ὁ ὄχλος
ἦλθαν ... ἵνα .. ἴδωσιν Περίχωρος Ἰερουσαλήμ (יְרוּשָׁלַיִם ךְלֶפ) occurs Neh.
iii 9, 12 ; comp. Acts xiv. 6 Δέρβην
καὶ τὴν περίχωρον. 'Joseph's Garden'
is according to Peter outside the
city, yet within a Sabbath day's
journey

5. τῇ δὲ νυκτὶ ᾗ ἐπέφωσκεν ἡ κυρια-
κή] With the exception of the incident just related, the Sabbath hours
of daylight are passed by without
remark, as in the canonical Gospels.
The thread of the story is taken up
again on Saturday night. Comp.
Matt. xxviii 1 ὀψὲ δὲ σαββάτων τῇ
ἐπιφωσκούσῃ εἰς μίαν σαββάτων. The
other Gospels represent the Sabbath
as past, as it was in fact when the
women arrived (Mk. διαγενομένου τοῦ
σαββάτου, L. τῇ δὲ μιᾷ τῶν σαββά-

των). For ἡ κυριακή=ἡ μία τῶν
σαββάτων see Apoc. 1 10 ἐγενόμην ἐν
πνεύματι ἐν τῇ κυριακῇ ἡμέρᾳ (where
however the sense is disputed).
Didach. 14 κατὰ κυριακὴν δὲ Κυρίου
συναχθέντες κλάσατε ἄρτον Ign.
Magn 9 μηκέτι σαββατίζοντες, ἀλλὰ
κατὰ κυριακὴν ζῶντες. In Barnabas
15 the day is ἡ ἡμέρα ἡ ὀγδόη, in
Justin apol 1 67 ἡ τοῦ ἡλίου λεγομένη,
but Barnabas is contrasting the eighth
day with the seventh, and Justin's
words are addressed to pagan readers
It is noticeable that as Peter uses
the term, an anachronism is involved.
The Didascalia avoids this error,
v. 14 τῇ νυκτὶ τῇ ἐπιφωσκούσῃ τῇ μιᾷ τῶν
σαββάτων Comp on the other hand
Ev. Nicod. 1. (B) 12, where the Jews
say to Joseph, Τῇ κυριακῇ πρωΐ θανάτῳ
παραδοθήσῃ Zahn remarks (p. 19).
"die feste Ausprägung des Namens ἡ
κυριακή tritt uns völlig klar und sicher
erst in dem Titel einer Schrift Melitos
περὶ κυριακῆς (Eus. iv. 26. 2) und in
den Leucianischen Apostelgeschich-
ten."

φυλασσόντων τῶν στρατιωτῶν ἀνὰ
δύο δύο] The κουστωδία consists of
eight men and the centurion. In
Acts xii. 4 there are sixteen (τέσσαρ-
σιν τετραδίοις), but eight of the whole
number are required to guard the
prisoner's person (6) ; here it is
enough to provide two sentries at
the door for each watch. Ἀνὰ
δύο δύο is a mixture of two con-
structions, which is admitted by

μεγάλη φωνὴ ἐγένετο ἐν τῷ οὐρανῷ καὶ εἶδον ἀνοιχθέν-
τας τοὺς οὐρανοὺς καὶ δύο ἄνδρας κατελθόντας ἐκεῖθεν,
πολὺ φέγγος ἔχοντας, καὶ ἐγγίσαντας τῷ τάφῳ. ὁ δὲ
λίθος ἐκεῖνος ὁ βεβλημένος ἐπὶ τῆ θύρᾳ ἀφ᾽ ἑαυτοῦ
5 κυλισθεὶς ἐπεχώρησε παρὰ μέρος, καὶ ὁ τάφος ἠνοίγη
καὶ ἀμφότεροι οἱ νεανίσκοι εἰσῆλθον. ἰδόντες οὖν
οἱ στρατιῶται ἐκεῖνοι ἐξύπνισαν τὸν κεντυρίωνα καὶ
τοὺς πρεσβυτέρους, παρῆσαν γὰρ καὶ αὐτοὶ φυλάσ-
σοντες· καὶ ἐξηγουμένων αὐτῶν ἃ εἶδον, πάλιν ὁρῶσιν
10 ἐξελθόντας ἀπὸ τοῦ τάφου τρεῖς ἄνδρας, καὶ τοὺς δύο

1 ανοιχθεντες   2 εκειθε   4 λειθος | εκειν[ος]   5 κυλ[ισθεις]|
ἐπεχώρησε] ἀνεχώρησε H., ὑπεχώρησε R, Z | ἠνοίγη] ενοιγη last syllable
uncertain, the word may have been longer   6 ιδ[οντες]   7 κ[εντυ]|ριωνα
8 αὐτοὶ] The heliotype is indistinct   αν οι B, αὐτοὶ R., H, L, Z ; Redpath
conjectures ἄλλοι   9 ορασιν   10 εξελθοντες | ανδρες

W. H. as a primary reading in Luke
x. 1, where it stands in BK. It
occurs also in *Acta Philipp.* 36
βαδίζουσαι ἀνὰ δύο δύο. Κατὰ
φρουράν seems to=κατὰ φυλακήν 'for
each watch of the night'; for φρουρά
in this sense comp. Herodian. iii. 11.

1. μεγάλη φωνὴ ἐγένετο ἐν τῷ οὐρανῷ]
Apoc. xi. 15 ἐγένοντο φωναὶ μεγάλαι.
xii. 10 ἤκουσα φωνὴν μεγάλην ἐκ τοῦ
οὐρανοῦ. The rest of the imagery is
also apocalyptic : comp Ezek. i. 1
ἠνοίχθησαν οἱ οὐρανοί Apoc xxi 10,
11 ἔδειξέν μοι τὴν πόλιν τὴν ἁγίαν κατα-
βαίνουσαν ἐκ τοῦ οὐρανοῦ ἔχουσαν τὴν
δόξαν τοῦ θεοῦ ὁ φωστὴρ αὐτῆς κ.τ.λ.
Πολὺ φέγγος ἔχοντας may have formed the end of a hexameter in some
Christian poem (cf. J. R Harris,
Cod Bez. p. 49). For
δύο ἄνδρας comp. Luke xxiv. 4
ἰδοὺ ἄνδρες δύο ἐπέστησαν αὐταῖς (the
women). Mt. relates the descent,
but limits it to one (ἄγγελος γὰρ
Κυρίου καταβὰς ἐξ οὐρανοῦ.. ἦν δὲ
ἡ εἰδέα αὐτοῦ ὡς ἀστραπή)   The
two soldiers on guard find themselves suddenly confronted by two

dazzling members of the στρατιὰ
οὐράνιος.

3. ὁ δὲ λίθος ἐκεῖνος κ τ λ] 'The
stone above mentioned' (cf. *infra*
οἱ στρατιῶται ἐκεῖνοι xi τὸν σταυρωθέντα ἐκεῖνον. Pet. *Apoc.* τοῦ βορβόρου
ἐκείνου)   In Mt the Angel rolls
away the stone, cf Mk. (ἀποκεκύ-
λισται), L. (ἀποκεκυλισμένον), P. represents it as moving of its own
accord   Comp. Acts xii. 10 τὴν
πύλην τὴν σιδηρᾶν ἥτις αὐτομάτη ἠνοίγη
αὐτοῖς (although an Angel is present
to whom the task might have been
assigned). Ὁ τάφος ἠνοίγη cf. *infr.* c.
xi 29 εὗρον τὸν τάφον ἠνεῳγμένον, Matt.
xxvii. 52 τὰ μνημεῖα ἀνεῴχθησαν. Οἱ
νεανίσκοι εἰσῆλθον comp Mark xvi.
5 εἰσελθοῦσαι εἰς τὸ μνημεῖον εἶδον
νεανίσκον.

8. παρῆσαν γὰρ καὶ αὐτοὶ φυλάσ-
σοντες] Sc οἱ πρεσβύτεροι Comp
c. x. τὸν τάφον ὃν ἐφύλασσον, where,
although οἱ περὶ τὸν κεντυρίωνα are
named, the context shews that 'the
Jews' are intended

10. τρεῖς ἄνδρας κ τ λ.] They had
seen two men enter   Comp Dan iii.

τὸν ἕνα ὑπορθοῦντας, καὶ σταυρὸν ἀκολουθοῦντα αὐ-
τοῖς· καὶ τῶν μὲν δύο τὴν κεφαλὴν χωροῦσαν μέχρι

1 ακολοθουντα

24, 25. The Third is 'supported' by
the two, but the support appears to
be regarded as nominal only, since
He is also said to be 'conducted'
(*infra*,χειραγωγουμένου). The very rare
word ὑπορθοῦν was used by Symm. in
the phrase τὰ ὑπορθοῦντά με = יְשַׁעַי
(Ps. xliii 19, lxxii. 2). With this
vision of the three, comp. the addition to Mark xvi. 3 in the O. L cod.
Bob (*k*) "descenderunt de caelis
angeli, et surgent[es] in claritate
uiui dei simul ascenderunt cum
eo" The *Ascension of Isaiah* describes a similar vision "descensus
angeli ecclesiae Christianae quae in
caelis est et angeli (? angelus) Spiritus
Sancti et Michaelis angeli (? Michael
angelus) angelorum sanctorum, et
ὅτι tertio die aperuit sepulchrum
eius, et dilectus ille sedens super
humeros seraphin exibit."

1. καὶ σταυρὸν ἀκολουθοῦντα αὐ-
τοῖς] In *Ev. Nicod.* ii. 10 the penitent
λῃστής appears in Paradise βαστάζων
ἐπὶ τῶν ὤμων αὐτοῦ καὶ σταυρόν. The
Lord's Cross 'follows' Him, endued
with a quasi-personality. See Didron,
Iconographie chrétienne, p. 375 ff. "la
croix est plus qu'une figure du Christ;
elle est, en iconographie, le Christ
lui-même ou son symbol"; and comp.
his remarks on 'the Cross of the
Resurrection,' *ib.* p 393 ff. Comp
Zahn, *Acta Joannis*, p. 223 (*fragm* 2)
ὁ σταυρὸς ὁ τοῦ φωτὸς ποτὲ μὲν λόγος
καλεῖται ὑπ' ἐμοῦ δι' ὑμᾶς, ποτὲ δὲ νοῦς,
ποτὲ δὲ Χριστός, ποτὲ θύρα, ποτὲ ὁδός,
ποτὲ ἄρτος, ποτὲ σπόρος, ποτὲ ἀνάστασις,
ποτὲ Ἰησοῦς, ποτὲ πατήρ, ποτὲ πνεῦμα,
ποτὲ ζωή, ποτὲ ἀλήθεια, ποτὲ χάρις.
Malan, *Conflicts of the Apostles*, p 9.
St Peter going up to the cross on
which he is to suffer addresses it

thus. "In the name of the Cross, the
hidden mystery, the grace ineffable..
Jesus Christ.. is the Tree of the Cross,
the cleansing of men," &c. The acros-
tics in the Sibylline Oracles, viii.
217 ff., where thirty-four lines begin with the consecutive letters of
Ἰησοῦς Χρειστὸς θεοῦ υἱὸς σωτὴρ σταυρός, indicate a similar identification
of the Cross with the Crucified.
It is noteworthy that in quoting the
passage Augustine (*civit. Dei* xviii.
23) excludes the σταυρός lines. They
run as follows.

Σῆμα δέ τοι τότε πᾶσι βροτοῖς σφρη-
γὶς ἐπίσημος,

Τὸ ξύλον ἐν πιστοῖς, τὸ κέρας τὸ πο-
θούμενον ἔσται,

Ἀνδρῶν εὐσεβέων ζωή, πρόσκομμα δὲ
κόσμου,

Ὕδατι φωτίζον κλητοὺς ἐν δώδεκα
πηγαῖς

Ῥάβδος ποιμαίνουσα σιδηρείη γε κρα-
τήσει.

Οἷτος ὁ νῦν προγραφεὶς ἐν ἀκρο-
στιχίοις θεοσήμοις

Σωτὴρ ἀθάνατος βασιλεύς, ὁ παθὼν
ἕνεχ' ἡμῶν.

The Valentinian schools used Σταυρός as a synonym for Ὅρος, the limit
of the πλήρωμα Iren. i. 3. 5. Hippol.
vi. 31. Clem. Alex *exc.* § 42.

2. καὶ τῶν μὲν δύο τὴν κεφαλὴν
κ.τ λ] The colossal stature assigned
to the two Angels finds some precedent in Apoc. x. 1, 2, comp. *Anaph.
Pilati* (A) 9 ἄνδρες ἐφαίνοντο ὑψηλοί.
For the supereminent height ascribed
to our Lord comp. Phot. *bibl.* cod.
114 λέγει δὲ μηθ' ἐνανθρωπῆσαι ἀληθῶς
ἀλλὰ δόξῃ (edd. δόξαι) καὶ πολλὰ πολ-
λάκις φανῆναι τοῖς μαθηταῖς .. καὶ μεί-
ζονα καὶ ἐλάττονα καὶ μέγιστον, ὥστε
τὴν κορυφὴν διήκειν ἔσθ' ὅτε μέ-

τοῦ οὐρανοῦ, τοῦ δὲ χειραγωγουμένου ὑπ' αὐτῶν
ὑπερβαίνουσαν τοὺς οὐρανούς. καὶ φωνῆς ἤκουον ἐκ
τῶν οὐρανῶν λεγούσης Ἐκήρυξας τοῖς κοιμωμένοις· καὶ
ὑπακοὴ ἠκούετο ἀπὸ τοῦ σταυροῦ [ὅ]τι Ναί.

1 χειρατωτουμενου· χειραγωγ R., H., Z
κοιμωμένοις; R, Z., κοιμωμένοις. L.
4 ὅτι Ναί] τιναι appears in the heliotype
jectured τὸ Ναί

2 φωνη   3 κοινωμενοις.
3—4 καὶ ὑπακοὴ] ὑπακοήν; καὶ H.
ὅτι ναί R., H., L., Z.; I had con-

χρις οὐρανοῦ. Similarly in Hermas, *sim.* ix 6, the man who is afterwards identified with the Son of God is ὑψηλὸς τῷ μεγέθει ὥστε τὸν πύργον ὑπερέχειν. Hilgenfeld (on Heimas *l c*) adduces 4 Esdr ii. 43 "in medio eorum erat iuuenis statura celsus eminentior omnibus illis . et dixi angelo Ille iuuenis, quis est? . et respondens dixit mihi Ipse est filius Dei." Comp. the description of the angel from whom the Book of Elkesai purported to be a revelation, and who was said to be the Son of God (Hipp. ix. 13)

Dr C. Taylor (*Hermas and the Fourth Gospel*, p. 78) refers to Gen. xxviii. 12 [John 1 51], and compares the Talmudic first Adam Streane, *Chagigah*, p 58 "R El'azar said, The first man extended from the earth to the firmament . and inasmuch as he sinned, the Holy One .. placed His hand upon him and made him small " The Sinless Man would reassume the proportions of the progenitor of the race   Χειραγωγεῖν occurs in Acts ix. 8, xxii 11 (in reference to Saul)

2 καὶ φωνῆς ἤκουον κ.τ λ] Comp p. 17,l 1. This second voice from Heaven is audible John xii. 28, 29, 2 Pet. 1. 17, 18 Ἐκήρυξας τοῖς κοιμωμένοις is probably not a question addressed to the Cross, but the revelation of a fact It is natural to compare 1 Pet iii. 18 θανατωθεὶς μὲν σαρκὶ ζωοποιηθεὶς δὲ πνεύματι ἐν ᾧ καὶ τοῖς ἐν φυλακῇ πνεύμασιν πορευθεὶς ἐκήρυξεν · ib iv 6 καὶ νεκροῖς εὐηγγελίσθη. Κοιμωμένοις

was perhaps suggested by τῶν κεκοιμημένων ἁγίων in Matt. xxvii. 52; the resurrection of 'the Saints that slept' is regarded by Euseb *d. e.* 500 as a result of the Descent.—for the pres. part. comp 1 Thess. iv. 13 περὶ τῶν κοιμωμένων (so אBA &c.). For early references to the Preaching in Hades see Bp Lightfoot's note on Ign. *Magn.* 9; an apocryphal prophecy quoted by Justin (*dial* 72) and by Irenaeus (iii. 20 4 and elsewhere), and attributed to Jeremiah or Isaiah, is of special interest in this connexion ἐμνήσθη δὲ Κύριος ὁ θεὸς ἀπὸ [ν *l.* ἅγιος] Ἰσραὴλ τῶν νεκρῶν αὐτοῦ τῶν κεκοιμημένων εἰς γῆν χώματος [cf. Dan xii 2], καὶ κατέβη πρὸς αὐτοὺς εὐαγγελίσασθαι αὐτοῖς τὸ σωτήριον αὐτοῦ

4. ὑπακοὴ ἠκούετο κ τ λ] For ὑπακοή, a response or refrain, comp. Method. *conviv.* x virg 208 c τὴν Θέκλαν ἔφη .. κοσμίως ψάλλειν· τὰς δὲ λοιπὰς ἐν κύκλῳ καθάπερ ἐν χοροῦ σχήματι συστάσας ὑπακούειν αὐτῇ— after which the ὑπακοή follows at intervals. The verb is used in a similar sense in earlier Christian literature ; comp. Zahn, *A. J*, p. 220 ἡμεῖς κυκλεύοντες ὑπηκούσαμεν αὐτῷ τὸ Ἀμήν. *Mart. Barth* 7 ὑπήκουσαν τὸ Ἀμήν. *Dorm. Mariae* 44 ὑπήκουσαν τὸ Ἀλληλούια. See also Malan, *Conflicts of the Apostles*, p 9. Harnack corrects ὑπακοήν, and punctuates ἐκήρυξας τοῖς κοιμ. ὑπακοήν, καὶ ἠκούετο κ τ λ , supposing Peter to refer to 1 Pet iii 19. But a change is unnecessary, and the allusion improbable

2—2

X. Συνεσκέπτοντο οὖν ἀλλήλοις ἐκεῖνοι ἀπελθεῖν
καὶ ἐνφανίσαι ταῦτα τῷ Πειλάτῳ. καὶ ἔτι διανοου-
μένων αὐτῶν φαίνονται πάλιν ἀνοιχθέντες οἱ οὐρανοὶ
καὶ ἄνθρωπός τις κατελθὼν καὶ εἰσελθὼν εἰς τὸ μνῆμα.
ταῦτα ἰδόντες οἱ περὶ τὸν κεντυρίωνα νυκτὸς ἔσπευσαν 5
πρὸς Πειλᾶτον, ἀφέντες τὸν τάφον ὃν ἐφύλασσον,
καὶ ἐξηγήσαντο πάντα ἅπερ εἶδον, ἀγωνιῶντες μεγά-
λως καὶ λέγοντες Ἀληθῶς υἱὸς ἦν θεοῦ. ἀποκριθεὶς
ὁ Πειλᾶτος ἔφη Ἐγὼ καθαρεύω τοῦ αἵματος τοῦ

4 κατελθον   5 κεντυρωνα   7 ἀγωνιῶντες] απανιωντες ἀγων. R., H., L., Z.

"Οτι Ναί is printed above as
nearer to the MS. than τὸ Ναί
which I had previously given. The
Classical Review (vii 1—2, p 42)
quotes a parallel from Lord Bute's
Coptic Morning Service; at the
kiss of peace in the liturgy, in
answer to the deacon's exhortation
Ἀσπάζεσθε ἀλλήλους ἐν φιλήματι ἁγίῳ,
the congregation answer Κύριε, ἐλέη-
σον (thrice)· ναί, Κύριε. A similar
response occurs in the *Acta Joannis*,
p. 239 Comp also 2 Cor. 1 20
ἐν αὐτῷ τὸ Ναί· διὸ καὶ δι' αὐτοῦ τὸ
Ἀμήν. The whole sentence suggests
that the preceding words ἐκήρυξας
κ.τ λ. belong to a hymn oi other liturgical form.

1. συνεσκέπτοντο οὖν ἀλλήλοις κ τ λ.]
Ps. ii. 2 Symm. ὕπαρχοι συνεσκέπτοντο
ὁμοθυμαδόν For ἐνφανίζειν, ' to make
an official report,' comp. Acts xxiii.
15, 22, xxiv. 1, xxv. 2, 15.

3. πάλιν.. ἄνθρωπός τις κατελθὼν]
Peter distinguishes between the descent of the two Angels (ἄνδρες δύο,
Luke xxiv. 4, δύο ἀγγέλους, John xx. 12)
and the descent of the one (ἄγγελος
Κυρίου καταβάς, Matt. xxviii 2, νεανίσκον, Mark xvi. 5). The incidents are
distinguished by Tatian also, but he
places them in the reverse order.
For εἰσελθών, see above on c. ix.

5 οἱ περὶ τὸν κεντυρίωνα] *Sc.* οἱ πρεσ-

βύτεροι or οἱ Ἰουδαῖοι, not the soldiers;
comp *infr.* ὑμῖν δὲ τοῦτο ἔδοξεν. Up
to this time they had not left the tomb
(ἐφύλασσον, cf c ix). Ἐξηγήσαντο, comp. Luke xxiv. 35, Acts x. 8,
&c. Ἀγωνιῶντες, cf c. v.
Ἀληθῶς υἱὸς ἦν θεοῦ is the confession of the Centurion at the Cross
and his soldiers (οἱ μετ' αὐτοῦ) in Mt ,
Mk (ἀληθῶς θεοῦ υἱὸς ἦν οὗτος =
ἀληθῶς οὗτος ὁ ἄνθρωπος υἱὸς θεοῦ ἦν)
Ephraim, probably referring to Tatian,
connects the words with the remorse
of the crowd (*uae fuit, uae fuit nobis,
filius Dei erat hic*), to the crowd
Peter has already assigned St Luke's
version of them

8 ἀποκριθεὶς ὁ Πειλᾶτος ἔφη κ.τ.λ.]
Comp Matt xxvii. 24. In Peter the
words possibly did not accompany
the symbolic washing, but were re-
served for this later juncture.
Ἀθῷός εἰμι ἀπό has been replaced by
the classical καθαρεύω. τοῦ υἱοῦ τοῦ
θεοῦ echoes back the confession of
the Jews, but answers to τοῦ δικαίου
τούτου which probably stood in the
text of Mt known to Peter; comp.
Ciasca, *Tatian*, p. 90. Ὑμεῖς
ὄψεσθε, which could not stand in
the altered position of the words, is
represented by ὑμῖν δὲ τοῦτο ἔδοξε =
'the sentence was yours, not mine'
comp. Matt. xxvi 66 τί ὑμῖν δοκεῖ,

υἱοῦ τοῦ θεοῦ, ὑμῖν δὲ τοῦτο ἔδοξεν. εἶτα προσελ-
θόντες πάντες ἐδέοντο αὐτοῦ καὶ παρεκάλουν κελεῦσαι
τῷ κεντυρίωνι καὶ τοῖς στρατιώταις μηδὲν εἰπεῖν ἃ
εἶδον· συμφέρει γάρ, φασίν, ἡμῖν ὀφλῆσαι μεγίστην
5 ἁμαρτίαν ἔμπροσθεν τοῦ θεοῦ, καὶ μὴ ἐμπεσεῖν εἰς
χεῖρας τοῦ λαοῦ τῶν Ἰουδαίων καὶ λιθασθῆναι. ἐκέλευσεν οὖν ὁ Πειλᾶτος τῷ κεντυρίωνι καὶ τοῖς στρατιώταις μηδὲν εἰπεῖν.

XI. Ὄρθρου δὲ τῆς κυριακῆς Μαριὰμ ἡ Μαγδα-
10 ληνή, μαθήτρια τοῦ κυρίου (φοβουμένη διὰ τοὺς Ἰουδαί-
ους, ἐπειδὴ ἐφλέγοντο ὑπὸ τῆς ὀργῆς, οὐκ ἐποίησεν ἐπὶ
τῷ μνήματι τοῦ κυρίου ἃ εἰώθεσαν ποιεῖν αἱ γυναῖκες
ἐπὶ τοῖς ἀποθνήσκουσι καὶ τοῖς ἀγαπωμένοις αὐταῖς),

1 ημιν   2 καιπερ εκαλουν   3 τω κεντωριων | μηδέν] μηδενὶ Ζ. | ἃ] ὧν
Blass   7 των κεντυριων   9 ορθου | Μαριαμ' | Μαγδαλινη   10 [ἥτις] φοβ. R.
12 ποιεν

For μηδέν it has been proposed to read μηδενί, but the change is perhaps unnecessary.

4. συμφέρει γάρ, φασίν, ἡμῖν κ.τ.λ.] For the construction comp Matt. v 29 συμφέρει γάρ σοι ἵνα ἀπόληται ἐν τῶν μελῶν σου καὶ μὴ ὅλον τὸ σῶμα βληθῇ εἰς γέενναν. John xi 50 συμφέρει ὑμῖν ἵνα εἷς ἄνθρωπος ἀποθάνῃ.. καὶ μὴ ὅλον τὸ ἔθνος ἀπόληται (cp. xviii. 14) But Peter can hardly mean to charge the Jews with the impiety of regarding a violent death as a greater evil than the extreme displeasure of God Probably, as Harnack suggests, he forgets that he has begun with συμφέρει, and intends to say 'to have incurred a grievous sin is enough, without being stoned besides' (das Eine ist schon genug Strafe). For ἐμπεσεῖν εἰς χεῖρας comp. Heb. x 31, and for the fear expressed by the Jewish leaders, Acts v. 26, ἐφοβοῦντο γὰρ τὸν λαὸν μὴ λιθασθῶσιν.

9 ὄρθρου δὲ τῆς κυριακῆς κ.τ.λ]

Luke xxiv 1 τῇ δὲ μιᾷ τῶν σαββάτων ὄρθρου βαθέως ἐπὶ τὸ μνῆμα ἦλθαν : ib. 22 γενόμεναι ὀρθριναὶ ἐπὶ τὸ μνημεῖον For τ κυριακῆς see note on p. 16, l 5.
The form Μαριάμ is well supported in John xx. 16, 18 and is the reading of אC in Matt. xxviii 1.   The N. T. has μαθήτρια only in Acts ix. 36. In Coptic Gnostic literature (Pistis Sophia, Second Book of Jeû), the μαθήτριαι correspond to the μαθηταί = ἀπόστολοι, and are headed by MaryMagdalene(Schmidt,Gnostische Schriften, p. 452).
10. φοβουμένη...αὐταῖς] The sentence is overweighted, and has fallen into grammatical confusion. I have followed Harnack's example in the provisional use of brackets, which makes it possible to construe without emending the text.   For φλέγεσθαι ὑπὸ τῆς ὀργῆς comp. φλ. ὑπὸ τῆς φιλοτιμίας, Dion Chrys i. p.158 The phrase is not in the N. T., but belongs to the literary style which Peter partly

λαβοῦσα μεθ᾽ ἑαυτῆς τὰς φίλας ἦλθε ἐπὶ τὸ μνημεῖον
ὅπου ἦν τεθείς. καὶ ἐφοβοῦντο μὴ ἴδωσιν αὐτὰς οἱ
Ἰουδαῖοι, καὶ ἔλεγον Εἰ καὶ μὴ ἐν ἐκείνῃ τῇ ἡμέρᾳ ᾗ
ἐσταυρώθη ἐδυνήθημεν κλαῦσαι καὶ κόψασθαι, καὶ νῦν
ἐπὶ τοῦ μνήματος αὐτοῦ ποιήσωμεν ταῦτα. τίς δὲ 5
ἀποκυλίσει ἡμῖν καὶ τὸν λίθον τὸν τεθέντα ἐπὶ τῆς
θύρας τοῦ μνημείου, ἵνα εἰσελθοῦσαι παρακαθεσθῶμεν
αὐτῷ καὶ ποιήσωμεν τὰ ὀφειλόμενα ; μέγας γὰρ ἦν ὁ
λίθος, καὶ φοβούμεθα μή τις ἡμᾶς ἴδῃ. καὶ εἰ μὴ δυνά-
μεθα, κἂν ἐπὶ τῆς θύρας βάλωμεν ἃ φέρομεν εἰς μνημο- 10
σύνην αὐτοῦ, κλαύσομεν καὶ κοψόμεθα ἕως ἔλθωμεν εἰς
τὸν οἶκον ἡμῶν. καὶ ἀπελθοῦσαι εὗρον τὸν τάφον ἠνεῳ-

4 κόψεσθαι | καὶ] κἂν H , Z. (after Blass)   8 οφιλομενα   11 κλαύσωμεν
καὶ κοψώμεθα R., H , Z   12 εὗρον] συρον

adopts. In καὶ τοῖς ἀγαπ. either καὶ
or τοῖς is superfluous. Ἀγαπ may
allude to Zech. xii 10 κόψονται. ὡς
ἐπ᾽ ἀγαπητῷ Τὰς φίλας· the Gospels
mention Μαρία ἡ Ἰακώβου, Σαλώμη,
Ἰωάνα ; and there were others who
are not named (L , αἱ λοιπαὶ σὺν αὐταῖς). In the Fourth Gospel Mary
Magdalene seems to be alone Ὅπου
ἦν τεθείς comp Luke xxiii 55 ἐθεά-
σαντο τὸ μνημεῖον, καὶ ὡς ἐτέθη τὸ
σῶμα αὐτοῦ Peter stands alone in
suggesting that fear had prevented
the women from ministering at the
tomb before the morning of Easter
day ; in the Synoptic Gospels they
return from the Burial to keep the
legal Sabbath-rest (Luke xxiii. 56),
and after the Sabbath is over they
are busy with preparations for their
work (Mark xvi. 1, Luke xxiv 1)
2. καὶ ἐφοβοῦντο μὴ ἴδωσιν αὐτὰς
κ τ λ] This seems to be an inference
from ὄρθρου βαθέως—they came at
break of day before sunrise, in order
to escape observation, cf. infra, l. 9
The canonical Gospels again are
silent as to the motive of fear , the

early visit to the tomb which they
report might have been prompted by
eager devotion. For κλαῦσαι καὶ κόψασθαι comp Luke viii 52 ἔκλαιον δὲ
πάντες καὶ ἐκόπτοντο αὐτήν Apoc. xviii.
9; infra, l 11
5. τίς δὲ ἀποκυλίσει κ τ.λ.] Mark
xvi 3 τίς ἀποκυλίσει ἡμῖν τὸν
λίθον ἐκ τῆς θύρας τοῦ μνημείου;
Εἰσελθοῦσαι occurs in Mk xvi. 5
(אACD). Παρακαθεσθῶμεν is perhaps
suggested by Luke x. 39 παρακαθισ-
θεῖσα πρὸς τοὺς πόδας τοῦ κυρίου .
comp also John xx 12 θεωρεῖ δύο
ἀγγέλους . . καθεζομένους . . ὅπου ἔκειτο
τὸ σῶμα Μέγας γὰρ ἦν ὁ λίθος
comp. Mk. xvi. 4 ἦν γὰρ μέγας σφόδρα
9 καὶ εἰ μὴ δύναμεθα κ.τ λ] 'If
we cannot execute our mission within
the tomb, we will bewail Him on the
way home , we shall not be content
with placing our offerings at the
door.' Ἃ φέρομεν=ἃ ἡτοίμασαν ἀρώματα (L)   For μνημοσύνη the LXX.
and Ν T. use μνημόσυνον (e g Matt.
xxvi. 13).
12. εὗρον τὸν τάφον ἠνεῳγμένον
κ τ.λ] Luke xxiv. 2 εὗρον τὸν λίθον

γμένον· καὶ προσελθοῦσαι παρέκυψαν ἐκεῖ, καὶ ὁρῶσιν ἐκεῖ
τινα νεανίσκον καθεζόμενον μέσῳ τοῦ τάφου, ὡραῖον καὶ
περιβεβλημένον στολὴν λαμπροτάτην, ὅστις ἔφη αὐταῖς
Τί ἤλθατε; τίνα ζητεῖτε; μὴ τὸν σταυρωθέντα ἐκεῖνον;
5 ἀνέστη καὶ ἀπῆλθεν· εἰ δὲ μὴ πιστεύετε, παρακύψατε
καὶ ἴδατε τὸν τόπον ἔνθα ἔκειτο, ὅτι οὐκ ἔστιν· ἀνέστη
γὰρ καὶ ἀπῆλθεν ἐκεῖ ὅθεν ἀπεστάλη. τότε αἱ γυναῖκες
φοβηθεῖσαι ἔφυγον.

XII. Ἦν δὲ τελευταία ἡμέρα τῶν ἀζύμων, καὶ

2 ἐν μέσῳ H., Z.   3—4 αυταιοτι   5 πιστευεται   6 εκει^{το}
8 φοβηθεισεφυγον

ἀποκεκυλισμένον. Matt. xxvii 52 τὰ
μνημεῖα ἀνεῴχθησαν   Παρέκυψαν
John xx 11 Μαρία   παρέκυψεν εἰς τὸ
μνημεῖον comp 1 Pet. 1 12 εἰς ὃ ἐπι-
θυμοῦσιν ἄγγελοι παρακύψαι. Ὁρῶσιν
.λαμπροτάτην Mark xvi 5 εἶδον
νεανίσκον καθήμενον . περιβεβλημένον
στολὴν λαμπράν
4 Τί ἤλθατε κ τ λ] Matt. xxviii.
5 ff. τὸν ἐσταυρωμένον ζητεῖτε οὐκ ἔστιν
ὧδε ἠγέρθη γάρ . . ἴδετε τὸν τόπον ὅπου
ἔκειτο Comp with Peter's version of
the Angel's words Εv Nιcod 1 (B)
13 οὐκ ἔστιν ὧδε ἀλλὰ ἀνέστη κύψατε
καὶ ἴδετε τὸν τάφον ὅπου ἔκειτο τὸ σῶμα
αὐτοῦ   The omission of ὧδε in
Peter finds a parallel in the S Ger-
main MS g² (non est, surrexit, Luke
xxiv 4). Ἀνέστη may have been
(as Dr Taylor points out) suggested
by Mark xvi 9 (ἀναστὰς δὲ πρωὶ
πρώτῃ σαββάτου ἐφάνη πρῶτον Μαρίᾳ
τῇ Μαγδαληνῇ) For παρακύψατε see
last note.

7. ἀπῆλθεν ἐκεῖ ὅθεν ἀπεστάλη] Mt ,
Mk , have προάγει ὑμᾶς εἰς τὴν Γαλι-
λαίαν ἐκεῖ αὐτὸν ὄψεσθε   Ἀπῆλθεν
in Peter seems to look back either to
ἀνελήφθη (c. v.) ; comp Constitutions
viii. 1 ἀνελήφθη πρὸς τὸν ἀποστείλαντα
αὐτόν) ; or to the exit from the tomb
described in c ix   For ἀπεστάλη see Matt x 40, xv 24, &c.,

and esp John xvi. 5, xx. 21.   In
Aphraates hom 22 (cited by Prof.
Robinson, Peter, p. 29 n), ed. Wright,
p ܩܡܠ, a similar saying is ascribed to the Angel at the tomb .

ܢܐܠ ܐܝܙܪ ܪܐܪܠܐ
ܠܝܪܐ ܐܠ ܡܢܐ ܡܝܐܠ
ܡܝܝܠܝ ܦܪ ܕܢܠ. The words
are not in the Arabic Tatian or in
Ephraim's commentary, but may have
stood, as has been suggested, in the
original Diatessaron on which "the
first 22 homilies [of Aphraates] are
based" (J R Harris, Tatian, p 19).
Cf Cyril. catech xiii 41 τὸν ἀποσταλέντα κύριον   τὸν ἀποστείλαντα πατέρα
θεόν

αἱ γυναῖκες φοβηθεῖσαι ἔφυγον] Mark
xvi 8 ἔφυγον ἀπὸ τοῦ μνημείου .
ἐφοβοῦντο γάρ. Mt represents the
fear of the women as mixed with joy
(μετὰ φόβου καὶ χαρᾶς μεγάλης).

9. ἦν δὲ τελευταία ἡμέρα τῶν ἀζύμων]
If Peter is following Jewish reckoning, he passes abruptly from Easter
day to the Friday in Easter week
(Nisan 21) M Lods however suggests (p. 21) that Peter has here
transferred Christian ideas to the
Jewish feast, and has called Easter-day

πολλοί τινες ἐξήρχοντο, ὑποστρέφοντες εἰς τοὺς οἴκους
αὐτῶν τῆς ἑορτῆς παυσαμένης. ἡμεῖς δὲ οἱ δώδεκα
μαθηταὶ τοῦ κυρίου ἐκλαίομεν καὶ ἐλυπούμεθα, καὶ
ἕκαστος λυπούμενος διὰ τὸ συμβὰν ἀπηλλάγη εἰς τὸν
οἶκον αὐτοῦ. ἐγὼ δὲ Σίμων Πέτρος καὶ Ἀνδρέας ὁ 5
ἀδελφός μου λαβόντες ἡμῶν τὰ λίνα ἀπήλθαμεν εἰς
τὴν θάλασσαν· καὶ ἦν σὺν ἡμῖν Λευεὶς ὁ τοῦ Ἀλφαίου,
ὃν Κύριος * * *

2 παυσαμινης   7 θαλ|λασσαν   8 [ὁ] Κύριος R, Z.

'the last day of the feast of unleavened bread,' because it was regarded
as closing the Christian *pascha* On
the whole question see the Introduction, c. iv.
With τελευταία ἡμέρα comp John
vii 37 ἐν δὲ τῇ ἐσχάτῃ ἡμέρᾳ τῇ μεγάλῃ
τῆς ἑορτῆς. The return to their homes
of the visitors who had attended the
feast reminds us of Luke ii 43, 44
τελειωσάντων τὰς ἡμέρας ἐν τῷ
ὑποστρέφειν ἐν τῇ συνοδίᾳ.
2 οἱ δώδεκα μαθηταί] Comp John
xx. 24 Θωμᾶς δὲ εἷς ἐκ τῶν δώδεκα
1 Cor xv 5 ὤφθη Κηφᾷ εἶτα τοῖς
δώδεκα. An exact parallel occurs in
Pet. *apoc* ἡμεῖς οἱ δώδεκα μαθηταὶ ἐδεή-
θημεν (where, as Mr James points
out, the time is probably subsequent
to the Resurrection), see also Zahn,
Acta Joannis, p. 32 μετὰ τὸ ἀναστῆναι
αὐτὸν ἐφάνη ἡμῖν τοῖς δώδεκα ἀποστόλοις
αὐτοῦ. *Acta Thadd.* 6 ὤφθη καὶ ἡμῖν
τοῖς δώδεκα
3 ἐκλαίομεν καὶ ἐλυπούμεθα] See
supra, c. vii. With τὸ συμβὰν comp
Luke xxiv. 14 ὡμίλουν πρὸς ἀλλήλους
περὶ πάντων τῶν συμβεβηκότων τούτων
the word occurs also in 1 Pet. iv. 12,
2 Pet ii. 22. Ἀπηλλάγη κ τ λ. finds
a parallel in the *pericope de adult.*
which begins καὶ ἐπορεύθησαν ἕκαστος
εἰς τὸν οἶκον αὐτοῦ. The bond of co-
hesion was gone since the Master's
departure

5 ἐγὼ δὲ Σίμων Πέτρος] Similarly in
the *Constitutions (e g* ii 46, iv 7, v 7,
vi. 12, vii 11), St Peter is the speaker
when events in the Gospel history
are related in which he took a part.
The narrative upon which Peter
is about to enter is probably to be
identified with that of John xxi 1 ff ;
the scene is here as there ἐπὶ τῆς
θαλάσσης τῆς Τιβεριάδος. Ἦσαν ὁμοῦ,
St John begins, Σίμων Πέτρος καὶ Θωμᾶς . . καὶ Ναθαναὴλ . . καὶ οἱ τοῦ Ζεβε-
δαίου καὶ ἄλλοι ἐκ τῶν μαθητῶν
αὐτοῦ δύο Whether Peter proceeded
to name Thomas, Nathanael, James
and John, can be matter for conjecture only ; it is possible, as has been
suggested to me by Mr Wallis, that
he means to identify Andrew and
Levi with the ἄλλοι δύο in St John
Andrew is mentioned also by Nonnus, but the name of Simon Peter's
brother may have occurred to him
independently. Τὰ λίνα may be=τὰ
δίκτυα (Athenaeus 7, p. 284 B λίνα . .
ἔμπλεα), if we are to understand
'fishing lines,' comp. Matt. xvii 27
πορευθεὶς εἰς θάλασσαν βάλε ἄγκισ-
τρον.
8 ὃν Κύριος] We may supply ἐκάλε-
σεν καθήμενον ἐπὶ τὸ τελώνιον (Matt. ix.
9, Mark ii. 14), or, since Peter usually
departs from the precise wording of
the canonical Gospels, some equivalent phrase

TRANSLATION.

I. BUT of the Jews none washed his hands, neither Herod, nor any one of His judges, and since they did not choose to wash them, Pilate arose. And then Herod the king commandeth the Lord to be taken, saying unto them, What things soever I commanded you to do unto Him, do ye.

II. Now there stood there Joseph, the friend of Pilate and of the Lord, and knowing that they were about to crucify Him, he came to Pilate, and begged the body of the Lord for burial. And Pilate sent to Herod and begged His body, and Herod said, Brother Pilate, even if no man had begged Him, we should bury Him, inasmuch as the Sabbath draweth on, for it is written in the law that the sun set not on one that hath died by violence.

III. And he delivered Him to the people before the first day of unleavened bread, their feast So they took the Lord and pushed Him as they ran, and said, Let us hale the Son of God, since we have gotten power over Him. And they clothed Him with purple, and set Him on a seat of judgement, saying, Judge righteously, O King of Israel. And one of them brought a crown of thorns and put it on the head of the Lord, and others stood and spat upon His eyes, and others smote His cheeks; others pierced Him with a reed, and some scourged Him saying, With this honour let us honour the Son of God.

IV. And they brought two malefactors, and crucified the Lord in the midst of them, but He held His peace, as in no wise suffering pain. And when they had set up the cross, they placed on it the superscription, This is the King of Israel And they laid His garments before Him, and parted them, and cast lots upon them. But one of the malefactors upbraided them, saying, We have suffered thus for the ills that we wrought, but this man—what wrong hath He done you in that He became the Saviour of men? And they had indignation against him, and commanded that his legs should not be broken, to the end that he might die in torments.

V. Now it was midday, and darkness overspread all Judea, and they were troubled and distressed lest the sun had set, inasmuch as He was yet alive; it is written for them that the sun set not on one that hath died by violence. And one of them said, Give Him gall to drink with vinegar, and they mixed and gave Him to drink. So they accomplished all things, and filled up their sins upon their head. And many went about with lamps, supposing that it was night, and some fell And the Lord cried aloud, saying, My power, my power, thou hast left Me, and having said this He was taken up. And the same hour the veil of the temple of Jerusalem was torn in twain.

VI. And then they drew the nails from the hands of the Lord, and laid Him upon the earth, and the whole earth was shaken, and great fear came upon them Then the sun shone out, and it was found to be the ninth hour. But the Jews rejoiced, and they gave His body to Joseph to bury it, inasmuch as he beheld all the good things that He did. So he took the Lord and washed Him, and wrapped Him in linen and brought Him into his own tomb, called Joseph's Garden.

VII. Then the Jews and the elders and the priests, knowing what evil they had done to themselves, began to bewail and say, Woe to our sins! the judgement is at hand, and the end of Jerusalem. And I with my fellows was in sorrow, and being wounded at heart we hid ourselves, for we were sought for by them as malefactors and as minded to burn the temple, and besides all this, we were fasting, and we sat mourning and weeping night and day until the Sabbath.

VIII. But the Scribes and Pharisees and elders, being assembled together and hearing that the whole people murmured and beat their breasts, saying, If these exceeding great signs were wrought at His death, see how righteous He was—the elders were afraid and came to Pilate, beseeching him and saying, Deliver to us soldiers, that we may guard His sepulchre for three days, lest His disciples come and steal Him away, and the people suppose that He is risen from the dead, and do us mischief. So Pilate delivered unto them Petronius the centurion with soldiers to guard the tomb; and with them there came elders and scribes to the sepulchre, and having rolled a great stone against the centurion and the soldiers, all who were there together placed it at the door of the sepulchre, and they spread upon it seven seals, and pitched a tent there and kept guard Now when it was morning, at the dawning of the Sabbath, there came a crowd from Jerusalem and the country round about to see the sepulchre, how it had been sealed.

IX. Now on the night when the Lord's Day was drawing on, as the soldiers kept guard by two and two in a watch, there was a great voice in heaven, and they saw the heavens opened, and two men descend from thence with much light and draw nigh unto the tomb And the stone which had been cast at the door rolled away of itself and made way in part, and the tomb was opened, and both the young men entered in. The soldiers, therefore, when they saw it, awakened the centurion and the elders (for they were also there keeping watch), and as they told the things that they had seen, again they see three men coming forth from the tomb, two of them supporting the other, and a cross following them, and the head of the two reached to heaven, but that of Him who was led by them overpassed the heavens. And they heard a voice from the heavens, saying, Thou didst preach to them that sleep, and a response was heard from the cross, Yea.

X They took counsel therefore with one another to go and shew these things unto Pilate. And while they yet thought on this, the heavens again appeared to open, and a man descended and entered into the sepulchre. When they saw this, they of the centurion's company hastened by night to Pilate, leaving the tomb which they were guarding, and told all that they had seen, greatly distressed and saying, Truly He was the Son of God Pilate answered and said, I am clean from the blood of the Son of God, but this was your pleasure. Then they all came near and besought him, and entreated him to command the centurion and the soldiers to say nothing as to the things which they had seen, for it is expedient for us (they said) to be guilty of a very great sin before God, and not to fall into the hands of the people of the Jews and be stoned. Pilate therefore commanded the centurion and the soldiers to say nothing.

XI Now at dawn on the Lord's Day Mary Magdalene, a female disciple of the Lord—afraid by reason of the Jews, forasmuch as they were inflamed with wrath, she had not done at the sepulchre of the Lord what women are wont to do for those who die and who are dear to them—took with her her female friends, and came to the sepulchre where He was laid And they feared lest the Jews should see them, and they said, Although we could not weep and bewail Him on the day when He was crucified, let us do so now at His sepulchre. But who shall roll us away the stone which was laid at the door of the sepulchre, that we may enter in and sit by Him, and do the things that are due? for the stone was great, and we fear lest any man see us. And if we cannot, even though we should cast at the door the things which we bring for a memorial of Him, we will weep and bewail Him until we come to our house. So they went and found the tomb open, and they came near and stooped down to look in there; and they see there a young man sitting in the midst of the tomb, fair and clothed with a robe exceeding bright, who said to them, Wherefore are ye come? whom seek ye? Him Who was crucified? He is risen and gone   But if ye believe not, stoop down and look in, and see the place where He lay, that He is not here, for He is risen and gone thither from whence He was sent.   Then the women fled affrighted.

XII.   Now it was the last day of unleavened bread, and many went out of the city returning to their houses, the feast being at an end.   And we the twelve disciples of the Lord wept and were in sorrow, and every man withdrew to his house sorrowing for that which had come to pass. But I Simon Peter and Andrew my brother took our nets and went to the sea; and there was with us Levi the son of Alphaeus whom the Lord   *   *   *

I.

INDEX OF GREEK WORDS USED IN THE FRAGMENT.

An asterisk is prefixed to words not used, or used only in another sense, by N.T writers, a dagger to N.T. words which are not found in the Gospels; forms entirely new are denoted by uncial type The list is not exhaustive, common words, with no special interest attaching to their use, have not been registered.

II.

INDEX OF SUBJECT-MATTER.

www.ingramcontent.com/pod-product-compliance
Lightning Source LLC
LaVergne TN
LVHW021617080426
835510LV00019B/2613